DRIVEN x PURPOSE

Brandon M Egbert

Dedication

To my corner, who never counted me out or wavered in support, encouragement, prayer and so much more. None of this would have been possible without you.

About the Author

Brandon, the founder of *d_X_P Academy*, has lived a life defined by profound questions and a relentless pursuit of purpose. From an early age, he was driven by an innate curiosity about the greater meaning of life and a determination to rise above the ordinary. His journey was marked by moments of deep introspection and soul-searching, where he grappled with his identity and role in a seemingly indifferent world. Growing up, Brandon often found himself overwhelmed by the complexities and demands of life.

The weight of uncertainty about his path frequently left him feeling lost and despondent. Despite these trials, he remained steadfast in his quest for clarity and direction. His journey was characterized by an unwavering commitment to finding his true calling and making a meaningful impact.

During these trying times, it was his unshakable faith that provided a beacon of hope. Brandon turned to his spiritual beliefs, seeking solace and guidance. In moments of quiet reflection and prayer, he found a glimmer of hope that began to dispel his fears and doubts. He realized that faith was not merely a comfort but a powerful force that could illuminate a path through the darkest valleys of despair.

God's light, as Brandon often describes it, became a guiding force in his life. It was this divine presence that helped him navigate the turbulent waters of his existence. With each hardship, he learned invaluable lessons about the power of persistence, resilience, and the importance of believing in something greater than oneself. His faith became a wellspring of strength, enabling him to overcome obstacles that once seemed insurmountable.

As he continued on his journey, Brandon discovered his true calling. The struggles and trials he faced were not in vain; they were shaping him into a person of purpose and conviction. He found that each challenge reinforced his belief in the transformative power of faith. This newfound understanding propelled him forward, giving him the courage to pursue his dreams and aspirations.

Today, Brandon stands as a testament to the strength that comes from enduring life's hardships with faith as a guiding star. He is stronger and more whole, having discovered his role in the grand tapestry of life with God as his constant companion. His journey is not just a personal narrative but a universal story of hope and resilience. It is a reminder that even in the toughest times, faith can lead to profound personal growth and fulfillment.

In this book, Brandon shares his remarkable story with the hope of inspiring others who may be facing their own challenges. Through his experiences, he aims to offer a message of encouragement and affirmation: that faith can be a powerful ally, guiding individuals to find their place and purpose in the world. He believes that no matter how daunting the obstacles, a steadfast belief in the divine can illuminate the path to a brighter, more meaningful future.

Symphony Behind The Shadows

In the depths of despair, a dad did dwell,
His dreams once vibrant, now a somber shell.
With empty pockets and questions profound,
He wandered life's maze, searching for higher ground.
Amidst the shadows, his purpose unclear,
He questioned his role in this world so severe.

With worries like mountains, his spirit did sag,
Yet, he clung to his faith like a tattered flag.
Through the darkest of nights, he whispered his plea,
To the heavens above, for guidance to see.
With a heart heavy-laden, burdened by strife, He sought God's
direction to navigate life.

In the quiet of dawn, a glimmer appeared,
A purpose emerging, dispelling his fears.
For God's light had shone through the depths of despair,
And revealed to this father a purpose to bear.

With each trial he faced, his faith did persist,
A flame in his soul through the darkest mist.
In God's plan, he found meaning and worth,
His purpose on Earth, his reason for birth.
Through hardships and struggles, he learned to believe,
That faith in the divine could help him achieve.

In the end, he emerged stronger and whole,
For with God as his guide, he'd discovered his role.
So, let his tale remind us when troubles descend,
That faith can be our anchor, our truest friend.
When we seek out our purpose, in God's loving grace,
Even in the hardest of times, we'll find our place.

By: Houston Egbert

Contents

Chapter 1: Setting Sail

This book is the reassurance I never had; one that I hope can be the life raft that helps you stay afloat. It is a compilation of advice I never received, thoughts I was never able to form, and lessons I had to learn the hard way with very little, if any, guidance.

Part of my life's purpose, as you'll soon read, is to help others conquer the stories they've been told over time that have shaped a reality that strays from God's true path for them. In my own life, I was on many occasions lost in the tangled mess of my mind; I couldn't see clearly as I spun through my existence.

 Now, I'm here to tell you that story of me so you can begin to rewrite the story of *you*.

We start at the beginning, and it's a rollercoaster of a ride that at times went completely off the rails; so hang on tight.

I was thinking about keeping this story simple, just hitting the highlights, but the truth is, that won't cut it. I want you to really feel the inner battle I went through, and I hope my story rings true with you. The battles, the challenges, and the victories I faced — they're not unique to me. You're here because you believe there's more to life, just like I do. My story is the same story that's been told a million times, just through a new character, and maybe a different perspective.

This journey started during one of the darkest times in my life. Well, I should say the realization of the journey. I'd been struggling for a long time with common deterrents like betrayals and desperate action, but those were just symptoms of a deeper drive for a purpose that wasn't aligned.

Back when I was a kid, I was a good-natured, obedient kid. Sure, I made the usual dumb kid moves, but I didn't get into anything too wild. As you'll soon find out, I saved the truly off-the-wall stuff for later in life.

I grew up in the church, and when I say, "grew up in," I'm talking Sunday morning, Sunday night, Wednesday night, and what felt like any other time the doors were unlocked. "The church," was the old-school Christian kind. You know, back when denominations ruled the world. I was completely immersed in it, bombarded with rules and religious dogma. That's where my inner struggle began.

At that time I was torn between my deep belief in Jesus and my disgust with everything else from the religious realm. Even as a young kid, I pushed back. I began questioning what I was being taught and started to become resistant to believing things just because others did.

I have an older brother and we grew up working on cars with our dad. We not only fixed cars up, but we ensured they looked good while doing it. Wheels, neons, exhausts, sound systems full of bass, spoilers – you name it, and we did it. The church that we attended looked down on us because our hobbies didn't fit their mold of "Godly men." We didn't follow the man-made rules that they were pushing down our throats, or their guidance advising us, "this is the way to God." They told us that by spending our money on these cars and the passions we had rather than the church, that we were sinning. These statements and beliefs we were surrounded by ultimately shaped our views of church, religion, and a true relationship with God. They drove my brother to later get a tattoo that means, "if sin is forever, then forever let us sin."

Even though I felt something about these beliefs didn't sit right, even though I searched and hoped for the truth, I suppressed my opinions and questions (as most youth do) and continued to mold into my family's and my community's expectations.

My limiting beliefs had already begun to form by the constant miseducation and contradicting direction that surrounded me growing up. Every turn, every decision, and every circumstance I made as a child and then as a teenager brought feelings of shame and guilt rooted in the teachings of traditional faith and conservative lifestyles. This is where some truly significant things had to happen for me on my unspoken journey to find my own faith.

Contesting the status quo, I was seeking to truly understand and establish my own faith. I knew there had to be more to my beliefs than just following a set path to God, and facing the consequences if I didn't. That didn't sound like a loving God to me. There was a fierce battle that started within me, a battle between knowing there was more out there and shaking off old beliefs that portrayed God as someone who'd punish me for straying from the path. This battle took various forms over the years, but I clung to my faith, which I'd found on my own and in a much greater way. My first job ever was working at my local roller rink when I was a Junior in High School. I thought it was the best job ever. When times were simple and fun, this is where my ex-wife and I began dating. We had known each other since the fifth grade but didn't start dating until we were seniors in high school.

After high school, I had to make a big choice: Bible college or the Air Force. I always felt passionate about my ability to make a difference in the world and was drawn to anything that could provide that fulfillment.

Still, a question churned in my mind, "do I go after my faith or after my dad's approval?"

Let me unpack this for a minute. From a very young age I didn't feel like I fit in, and I didn't feel like my family believed I was one of them. I was different in many ways, and this drove a desire to be seen and heard. Nothing life altering happened that I can recall putting me in a place where I felt left out, untrusted, or "less than," but the reality is that's exactly how I felt.

As my life went on, I can remember very distinct times around the dinner table or throughout our family routines where I was treated differently, and can recall events that solidified this feeling inside me; times where I was not given a chance to be seen, heard, or accepted. All of this animosity was placed upon my dad as my scapegoat. Not that he did anything specifically that I can recall, but he became the figurehead for the desire within me to be accepted.

That was on me, and I see it now. I wanted so much to be seen, for those closest to me to know who I really was, differences and all. I wanted to be acknowledged for bringing something to the table and accepted in my family despite being so different from my dad and my brother. Faith, for my dad, was not something shown or spoken of growing up. My mom was the one driving us to church whenever the doors were open, and my struggles with faith and with seeking approval collided in major ways. I felt that my dad disapproved of my religious beliefs, while the church, in turn, was directing me away from the influence of my father.

When the time came to choose - church ministry or military, I chose the more radical option to see if it would spark that sense of belonging I was so desperately missing by clinging to my faith.

Air Force it was.

Before I left for bootcamp, I got a tattoo of a cross. This was the very beginning of my outward contesting of what I had been engulfed in from this so-called religion for so long. This did not go over well with my parents or the church. In fact, it pissed a ton of people off and I joined my brother in believing that, "if this is what sin is, then I'm going to keep it up."

The last thing on the to-do list was to propose to my girl before heading out.

And off I went.

Chapter 2: The Shipwreck

Bootcamp was a blast for me. I don't recall any terrible stuff happening like you see in the movies, and the standard mind games didn't get to me. Basic training wrapped up after six weeks and my parents even flew in for the occasion. Since I signed up for Security Forces, I shifted over to the other side of Lackland Air Force Base for technical school. That was when I got my first cell phone – my folks gave it to me as a graduation gift. (Yeah, I'm old. We didn't have cell phones in elementary school like kids these days.)

As school was winding down, we started receiving our base assignments.

Where was I going?

To a God forsaken place called F.E. Warren Air Force Base in Cheyenne, Wyoming.

My time in the military was incredible in many ways. I had some amazing experiences and made lifelong friends and family. However, that nagging feeling that I wasn't actually being seen and that there had to be *more* still lingered.

After arriving at my new base, I got my future wife and I a place to live, and then we got married.

Living in that first apartment wasn't too wild. We did get our first pets there, a black cat named Baby and a Catahoula Leopard dog named Jax (that dog was something special.) My new bride and I got involved in the local church and helped with the youth group. We had our first child together and began to build the family we had always envisioned and been taught to desire.

While I was in that little apartment I was a Security Forces member, guarding our nation's most destructive resource – nuclear weapons. Going out to the field was a whole different experience. My schedule was a bit crazy – three days in the field, three days home, three days in the field, and six days home. After doing this for over a year, President Bush directed that all nuclear bases create a tactical response force to handle threats against the nukes. Deny, delay, and contain — these were the orders. I wanted in on that.

When I set my mind on something, I go for it. So, I applied for the team, passed a rigorous physical fitness test, interviewed with the TRF leadership, and made it through indoctrination. Before I officially became part of the team, they had to beat me in.

Yes, I mean that *literally*.

They suited me up in a red man riot suit, and the team took turns beating me while I couldn't hit back. Only then did I get my call sign, "Talon 16." That team was one I will never forget. We did some next-level stuff together and were a team of straight-up badasses.

This is the point in my life where my foundation began to crumble.

During this time in Wyoming, I went to sniper school and reconnected emotionally with an old girlfriend. Although no physical acts occurred, I had betrayed my vows to my wife by letting my interests stray. I got caught and the guilt consumed me. I shifted and put the blame on my wife for it all. I was lost and did not know which way was up.

The dominos began to fall.

I reached a point where I felt the need to seek out that "more" I was lacking and create it for myself. As this first domino fell it represented the opening of a door into looking in every place that I could find for it; places I shouldn't have, places that brought even more shame and guilt. I was stuck in my own vicious cycle. I was always moving, always struggling to stay afloat. At the time, I didn't realize that I was also trying to cover up, make amends for, or even replace the shame I had from the thoughts within my own mind. Every place I sought out, every thought that crossed my mind brought potential to lead me to what I saw could be my true purpose.

Then, I failed sniper school.

The unfortunate part is that skill-wise I shouldn't have; it was all due to an oversight in the requirements to attend the school. The training and knowledge needed prior to attending is extensive and the person assigned to be my spotter did not have it. I was an amazing shot and I loved every second of training and honing my skills. I was ready to serve my country and I was all in. God had other plans and He made that very clear by allowing me to fail. This was an absolute turning point for me. My failure broke the military path I had planned, leaving me lost and unsure of what to do next. As I didn't have a clear sense of purpose, I desperately looked for direction, but my efforts were lacking the leading hand of God. Instead, I got stuck in a cycle of self-determined desire because I thought that my own goals were the way to happiness. While I was trying to find meaning in my life, I ignored God's presence and used His name as an excuse for what I was doing. Once the failed sniper school fiasco settled down, I decided to leave the military.

"Now what?"

The military was my plan. It was *the* plan. Determined to quickly push forward and give the impression of an intentional existence, I decided to get my pastoral certificate. After all, that was the other career option I had considered after high school.

I decided that becoming a pastor would be well suited to me and help me evolve some of my leadership skills while also strengthening my faith and allowing me to truly help people. I loved talking and teaching, and I believed I was pretty damn good at it. It was perfect.

As I think back on all these changes encountered throughout my life, it is evident I've always been a sucker for new adventures. You could say I'm a bit of an adrenaline junkie. Anything that can seriously mess me up or even kill me – I'm all in. These adventures seemed to come easy for me.

What I discovered through the work that I have done is that part of my extreme "all in" nature comes from my internal battle to make profound decisions that affect who I am, and my personal growth on the inside. Over and over I found myself opting for the path of least resistance or taking extreme risks because I didn't want to make a decision that was connected to who I actually was. Deep down I always sought approval from others and would distract people from who I was with bold moves and actions on the outside: going into the military because that was what my family did; becoming a pastor to hide the discontentment and shame within me; working toward and getting a job where my dad worked to be accepted and valued even though that didn't fit who I felt I truly was; lying and cheating to distract from the truth that I did not feel like I belonged.

This survival behavior had me constantly question why I was here, what my purpose was, and if there was more to life. I'd often ponder this about my career, but later, it started applying to my marriage, too.

"Do I choose or stick around because it is safe? What's our purpose as a partnership? Surely, there's more than this, right?"

There is a lot more that went into this particular situation, but I want to stick to the battles within my mind.

As I stumbled through some incredibly painful and rough times that first year after training, I'd hear all these voices in my head, like a riot that constantly followed me. They'd say there's more to life, but it wasn't for me. They'd say my wife deserved better and that I was holding her back and pushing her down further. They'd say I wasn't enough or even worthy of being loved by someone.

I made a commitment to fight those voices and embrace the truth; I just didn't know what that was yet. God had made me a promise long ago that he would show me my path, and I was convinced that a breakthrough was on the horizon. I surrendered to God's plan for my life, embracing the brokenness that would uncover and heal my struggles. I surrendered to loneliness and actually feeling the emotions I felt, hoping and believing and doing the work to get to the root of them. I surrendered to who I really was and looked forward to getting to know *me*.

In hindsight, in my own way, I was trying to find my way back to God because I was ashamed of who I'd become. I was drowning in all the voices telling me I wasn't good enough. I was overwhelmed reflecting on my reality – failing the military, my marriage in turmoil, and guilt consuming my mind. I thought maybe becoming a pastor would heal me instantly.

It didn't.

Chapter 3: Into The Depths

I genuinely believe everything in life shapes who we become, and I am who I am today because of my experiences. At the time I exited the military, I was desperately searching for answers, for a reason, for *more*, and for my place in this world.

My desires were contradicting and I felt I was constantly searching for something that would click effortlessly and make my purpose clear. I felt there had to be more to my existence than what I had experienced up until that point. I felt like since I had failed in my career, at forming my identity, and even in my marriage, I was required to "make up" for it in every other possible area I could find. I felt inadequate and unworthy, as if my thoughts and beliefs were wrong because they didn't fit into how my life was portrayed on the outside or what others believed. I lived in a constant state of fear that I might not be usable by God anymore because my mistakes weighed so heavily on me.

Up until and during this transition I made mistakes – I lied, I cheated, all while telling myself I was finding my way closer to God. I was a walking contradiction and I knew it, but I didn't know how to make my actions match my conviction. I wanted to change the way things were done, to speak my truth about my beliefs and how I saw the world and God's love. I wanted to be a catalyst to bring God's love, power and miracles back to this world because to this day I feel we desperately need it.

Welcome to the warfare in my mind and heart.

During this season of searching, I became many things, almost like a chameleon. From the military to a pastor; later a personal trainer to a leader at a Fortune 500 company – and so many others in between. I was searching for that elusive gold at the end of the rainbow, or the ancient treasure buried deep in the jungle, but all I found were my footprints leading me down my own path, never reaching what I was searching for.

This instability in who I believed myself to be led me towards fates I couldn't have imagined, and clouded my judgment in ways beyond my comprehension. It turned me into someone I didn't recognize, someone I never wanted to be. I was living in a fog, barely feeling alive. It's definitely not an excuse for my actions – I want to be clear about that, *and* chaos was my reality. I was watching my life unfold from above. Not truly living it.

In 2010, I believe God spoke to me in a *very* real way. He told me and promised me that my life would become what I intended, what I envisioned, and what I believed. That my life would be one of influence and His power to be shown to the entire world.

How could this be when the reality of my life and the actions I kept falling into were so contradictory to this promise?

This experience led me to compare myself to David in the Bible; anointed to be king, but his story didn't lead him directly to the throne. He went through some tough times, hiding in a cave, fearing for his life, and doubting God's promise. It took seven long years, but that promise *finally* became a reality. I held tightly to this story. To this promise that my purpose would finally be made known to me. Even as I believed, I worked to force it in my own ways. Being driven by *my* purpose.

Back to the timeline.

After I finished my pastoral studies, the church we were involved with hired me. My wife and I were all in, even though they wanted me to run the children's program instead of the youth, which was our passion. We moved into an apartment on the third floor of this massive 90,000-square-foot church building. The pay was less than what I made in the military, but we didn't care. We made a great team despite our marital issues. We accomplished some amazing things and had a lot of fun leading our programs and our community. We continued to grow our own family with two more children and were the picture-perfect unit to all those on the outside looking in.

Still, my shame and guilt were relentless. They haunted me and screamed at me from within. I prayed for forgiveness and healing constantly. I was in a perpetual state of dissatisfaction, always wondering what life would look like if things were different and even if I wasn't married to the one I chose. Thoughts of giving up and running away from myself were a constant presence. I only came to my senses when my wall of shame finally crumbled.

Many things happened very quickly at this time, including a move back to our home state of Washington. Now, I was working at a retail store in addition to the church back home. I was successful at everything I did, moved up quickly at my retail job, and then... I fell into destructive thoughts and behaviors like never before. My internal struggles became so strong that they manifested into some extreme ways, including physical affairs. Through those few years of career-related success I worked hard, climbed the ranks, and was seen as a true leader, all while behind the closed doors of my mind, I was self-sabotaging. I believed I wasn't worthy of the life I envisioned and didn't deserve what I was living in. I created false narratives and drama over and over again where there was none. I even strived to make my wife leave me as if our marriage was the ultimate issue. I thought maybe if one big thing would come crashing down, my internal struggles would go away with the wreckage. (Even writing that statement brings a cringe to my heart.) My internal tug-of-war came out from the shadows that I had buried it in – so unsettled *and* full of faith at the same time. Once again I was doing exactly what I knew was wrong and full of hope and faith that God would turn it around because he loved me.

Trust had been broken in my marriage and I was slowly trying to rebuild it. I even got a big pinup tattoo of my wife on my side to prove I was committed and all-in. I wanted to show that I was "better" and back to being stable. After a while, life seemed to be getting back to normal, or at least I thought it was.

I may have made it a whole year before falling back into my vicious cycle.

I was all over the place, completely lost and blinded, desperately searching for someone or something to fill this void. I wanted to find a greater purpose, the meaning behind it all. Searching for that *one* thing that would fix it all. Believing that this magic pill was out there and knowing it wasn't simultaneously. It was ridiculous.

On the outside, everything looked great. I had a beautiful family, a good job that I always excelled at, people loved me, *and* I had a whole chaotic battle of a life on the side. I was doing good deeds to make up for my hidden actions and beliefs that were tormenting me. Deep down I was questioning why all this had to happen to me.

Why was I going through this hell?

I longed to be free from this turmoil, to make it all disappear.

Life continued in ruins within me, through selling our house and moving in with my mother-in-law, juggling church, work, coaching my kids' basketball and baseball, and even buying what we believed was our dream home – a farm.

My family called it "The Farm," and we turned it into just that.

Moving to The Farm was a major milestone for me. I thought I'd put an end to my ridiculous behavior, and it was then that the real white-knuckle ride began.

After we'd settled into the new house, we came upon the opportunity to buy a fitness studio. This was a dream of mine, or so I made myself believe, and my wife went along with it. Things started off well, but we soon noticed strange financial irregularities that just didn't add up. Nothing about that business made sense. I continued my job at the retail store to make ends meet, often bouncing between the two obligations multiple times per day. God was at work again, opening and closing doors in ways that show it was only Him.

At The Farm, I was busy building and maintaining the property 24/7. We built a chicken coop and added all sorts of animals to the mix – chickens, ducks, geese to protect them from eagles (yep, we lost a few in front of our kids, which was quite the day), pigs, horses, goats, rabbits – The Farm was taking shape. It was a lot of work. We even had to leave the church once because the neighbor called saying our pigs had escaped... again.

About a year after moving in, my best friend and brother-in-law moved his family nearby. I was ecstatic! We had some epic times together, working with horses, dealing with a destructive yet oddly friendly boar, building a fire pit, and turning the tack room into our first cigar lounge called, The Golden Doorknob.

I was promoted at work which shifted my hours to the second shift. As a result, my wife had to manage the fitness studio mostly on her own, which proved to be more challenging than we anticipated. We knew it was coming to an end and in hindsight I think we were just stalling until the lease ran out.

Why did God let us buy that business just to get our finances messed up again?

Well, we now know that this was the breaking point; the cry for help. The final mess-up just waiting for me to bring it all crashing down. I don't believe God makes bad things happen to us, but sometimes He allows them to get our attention when all else fails.

Life took an unexpected turn when I shifted to the second shift without the burden of the fitness studio to worry about. I had more time at The Farm before work, and during that time I prayed a lot. I would walk our land in the morning and on those daily walks on the five acres, something tugged at my heart. It became increasingly clear that I needed to come clean that my life had not been what I portrayed to those closest to me. In hindsight, this was me trying to sabotage the good place I had come to. There must be something wrong in my life, and if not, I'd make sure I created it.

One Thursday morning, I mustered the courage to ask my wife if we could get coffee before work. We drove to a local coffee stand and then to a nearby park. That's when I spilled the beans about all the mess in my life and mind, including all the acts of betrayal. I told her about my straying thoughts in our marriage, my lies, the facade I had been parading, and the all around tornado that was in my soul. She was rightfully furious, but sure enough, I felt better about coming clean. Peace came over me, but I struggled to identify if it was peace about the truth, or peace that I was finally about to face the consequences of who I had been. While I thought I was experiencing a moment of change, it was really a moment of comfort in the mess. Comfort and peace in my constant place of chaos. The real goal in my mind was to push everyone away because that's what I believed I deserved. Like so many people, I was accustomed to this place and I always found ways to seek it out.

I called in sick for work that day and the next. We spent those days together, trying to make sense of it all. At the time, we came up with a bunch of reasons for it, so we tried many things – therapy, date nights, getaways – believing they were some sort of magical solution.

Things did temporarily improve between us, but it was another layer covering up the root issues – more fraud, and illusions to hide the truth. Those days off and the coming weeks were tough, but I also shared my turmoil and secrets with my best friend and our pastor. Telling our pastor felt more like a punishment, but I did it anyway. Surprisingly, they were kind and showed me grace.

My wife and I continued to grow together and even embarked on our first big trip, which was incredible. I became a bit famous among the locals on that trip because of my tattoos. After the trip, we decided to renew our vows.

Can you see the pattern yet?

Throughout my life, big mess-ups occurred, and then *big* gestures to show change while no root was uncovered or addressed. A big event, then a big show, and the cycle continued. The actions themselves were not wrong, but they distorted reality and distracted everyone from the severity of why they had taken place in the first place.

The vow renewal, or "cover-up," party planning commenced. The renewal turned into quite the soiree with a DJ, great food, personalized vows, and even a baptism as a symbol of starting over. Immediately after the renewal we took our kids to Disneyland to celebrate with our family.

However again, it was more hype than true change – more fraud.

A few months after this party of new beginnings, the bottom completely gave way. My life utterly fell apart because of my own destructive tendencies. The cycle was not stopped, and this was the final straw.

I'm a pretty decent guy – just ask anyone except my wife. I've always been a leader and a damn good one. I can make split-second decisions in my career, but when it comes to making decisions and committing to myself, I freeze. I can't do it. Back then, sometimes instead of saying something I believed, I'd blame it on someone else like my counselor. I lacked confidence in myself, in who I was, who I wanted to be, and even in God to use me.

One night at church, my friend asked me how I was doing.

I said, "Okay," as my eyes welled up with tears. I was utterly broken, and he sensed it.

"Are you sure?" he asked as he pulled me aside.

I finally admitted, "No. I'm lost, alone, and broken."

He understood. He started speaking life into me, sharing his own battles. He recommended a book that would change my life: *How to Survive a Shipwreck*. In the book the author talks about how what happened and the actions you took are just the surface of the rock your ship hit; it's what's below the surface that needs to be uncovered, and it's terrifying. There is more to the story than just what can be seen.

My friend told me to surrender and not resist the truth, to choose what I'm willing to fight for. I did just that.

"To peer into the sea that threatens to swallow you whole, dive into the mouth of it and trust. You have to let God happen to you, which requires letting life happen to you all the way down. You cannot continue to flail your arms, beat against the sea, and damn the waves. You have to let yourself go all the way under, into the depths of God, into the depths of your own soul, into the depths of life itself."

-How to Survive a Shipwreck, pg. 23

The work began in my own life to find *me*. To find out what was behind my behavior and what I needed to put an end to it once and for all. Things started to change. My marriage was slowly rebuilding and I began to work alongside others in the same situations. I knew I was meant to help people and I believed maybe this was it.

If only that had been the end of the story.

Chapter 4: Perfectly Imperfect

Life has a lot of twists and turns that can happen at any time. Its purpose is not what happens to us but how we react. It's knowing and believing that there is so much more. It's learning the lesson and seeing the gift in every circumstance. Even through pain, struggles and limiting beliefs. God is always there, faith can always be found, and the truth is constantly waiting to be uncovered.

For me, I had a deep-seated need to be validated, even though my own views and societal expectations were at odds with each other. I looked for comfort in approval – from my dad, to my pastors, to my friends. I viewed this approval as a sign that my decisions were right. But as time went on, I learned that getting approval from outside sources had its limits and I began to see very clearly that my passions and desires for life and true purpose didn't line up with the people I sought approval from.

Think about the stories we've heard from the Bible about people like Moses, David, and Paul. Each of them was flawed in some way, but God picked them to do something bigger. We can relate to their struggles because we have all been flawed and had doubts. They tell us that even when things look the worst, there is hope and redemption.

When things go wrong, or we don't know what will happen next, faith tells us to trust in something bigger than ourselves and to believe that everyone has worth, flaws and all. Being sure of this gives us comfort and strength because we know that our flaws are not obstacles to greatness, but rather chances to grow and change.

Remembering that God has a plan for each of us that is full of meaning and hope is needed for when we start to doubt ourselves and wonder if we are worthy. May this unchanging truth give us the strength to accept our flaws and aim for greatness, knowing that we are loved and valued.

As I look back on my life, I realize there were times when I thought I was doing what God wanted me to do and living out His plan for me, but now I see that most of the time it was just my own plans and dreams that led the way. I would tell myself that my successes were part of God's plan, but when things didn't go as planned, I would be let down. When I failed at something, I moved on to the next endeavor instead of trying again – and this would happen over and over again. I had a strong belief that God would use all of these failures to lead me to His real purpose for my life, even though they were difficult. He must have known I would trip and was using those lessons to get me ready for something bigger.

I believe that God shapes us through our problems so that He can carry out His bigger plan. No matter how hard things get, they are only steps on the way to learning and accepting His intention for our lives. So, even though things go up and down, I keep going because I know that God will lead me where I need to go. Things may get hard sometimes, but I have faith that His light will always be there to guide me to my true purpose.

I've always felt different. I *am* different. Cut from a different cloth; molded with a different batch of clay. Maybe this cloth was stained and maybe this batch of clay wasn't the right consistency for most, but I truly believe that while God was creating, He purposely stopped and set aside the clay he was using to grab the specific batch he needed for me; to mold me into exactly what I am today to fulfill the greatest calling and perfect purpose. This understanding is what has given me the greatest freedom in life; the ultimate release of control and need for validation and approval.

I am perfectly made.

Real happiness and genuine joy don't come from trying to please other people. They don't come from being someone you aren't. They don't come from pretending or hiding. They come from aligning with a higher purpose — a destiny that is driven by something bigger than what society expects of you.

While I was embracing this idea, I was freed from the chains of seeking approval from other people because I realized I was already approved by the one who created me.

I am perfectly imperfect.

Chapter 5: "Purpose"

You know that gnawing feeling deep inside you that screams, something's missing?

You're doing everything you know how to do – everything this world tells you to do, all the tricks and tips to bring fulfillment in your life; checking every box you could ever find in those Google searches and self-help books – but the emptiness prevails.

That's the discontent and the emptiness I was striving to fill.

Society tells us how to go after filling this void but after doing all they say we must, our souls are still hungry. This world of purpose, in my opinion, has been twisted and resold into something we don't even recognize anymore, and yet, we are still pursuing it. We are still making the choice to believe that we can force, fight, create, buy, run over, or build what is missing inside of us all on our own.

This is all about *purpose*. Real, God-given purpose. The idea that, anything other than our true purpose, can fill the void within us is a lie that has been ordained with glitter and gold and sold worldwide.

I am here to say what you already know, that the topic of purpose has been talked about in every which way and has concealed the truth. What is being spoken about in the elite circles and the influencer realms of this time is an illusion.

The journey to true purpose isn't what we think it is or what we have been made to believe. We've been misled into believing that being driven by purpose is all about getting ahead and running over anyone in our way. Look at most big name influencers or public figures within the business world and you will be taught that money brings purpose. They may even imply you have to be a complete dick to everyone to get noticed, beat out the competition, get rich, and be who you want to be. I am pretty sure we don't get up every morning thinking, "how many people can I screw over today?" – but that is one of the mindsets that is being preached every single day. It is what is shown to us by people in leadership who are supposed to have the greater good as their first priority.

We've heard various mantras a million times and in a billion different ways: *"hustle and grind, or you'll never get ahead."*

I understand the portion of this that is true. We must put in the work to get what we want. We have to be committed to long days and sacrifice. We have to be willing to do things differently. However, stating the importance of grit and audacity in this way is misleading. It advocates for burnout, discontentment, and neglect of anything and everything that doesn't contribute to money or success. What people actually get from this "grind mindset" is that being constantly busy defines having a purpose.

This mentality is exactly where most of us are and what my story showed. We are applauded for filling our lives with stuff, activities, and jam-packing our calendars. From personal experience, I can tell you that this is not the way to purpose. We are told what we must *do* to achieve a fulfilled and extraordinary life filled with the abundance we have *earned*. That we *worked* for. That we *deserve*.

But what's it really getting us?

A never-ending treadmill of exhaustion and the illusion that we are making progress and living in our purpose. *They* want us to believe that our purpose lies in the *more*. Doing more; having more. I'd suggest that having more is not a bad thing, but it's not the "more" that we need to focus on. "More" will not bring our purpose or fill any voids in our life.

I know you have noticed yourself scrolling through your social media feeds just to see everyone posting their highlight reel; the filtered version of their lives that looks nothing like reality – or at least *your* reality. We see their perfectly posed travel selfies, the shiny sports cars, the expensive gourmet meals, and the epic parties. While these things can be extremely enjoyable and great memories to be made, they are not *purpose*. The world today has redefined "purpose" as *stuff* and a busy calendar. We have allowed a true calling and purpose to be redirected into a *thing*. This new definition creates chaos in every part of us.

Today, a fear of missing out (FOMO) is the name of the game. We see our friends "living their best lives," and suddenly our own life seems mediocre in comparison. We're trapped in a never-ending cycle of chasing the next big thing, adding more to our daily grind, and thinking it's our path to purpose.

It's not.

We're wasting our precious time and energy on staying stuck in the cycle.

Our culture's definition of purpose is recognized by checking boxes and running people over to get ahead. We are told we must be at the front of the pack, no matter what it takes to get there. Once we achieve anything, we are told to help others do the same (for a fee, of course) and that then *that* will be what gives us purpose. Doing things in the name of helping people, but in reality helping our own bank accounts. Helping others is rarely only about the people being served.

That doesn't sound like what God literally created us to do and be.

In this book, I want to dismantle these misconceptions and pave the way for a revelation of what "purpose" truly means – my revelation that took decades of painful, messy mistakes to uncover.

Many of us are yearning for something beyond the daily grind. It's like we're wired for adventure, for meaning, but society keeps handing us a menu of distractions. We're swiping through life, trying to find that elusive "more" that's been missing.

I have come to realize that the disconnect between society's definition of purpose and our inner cravings is taking a toll on our mental health. Depression and anxiety are skyrocketing like an epidemic of lost souls. No wonder we are ready to jump when we're told to chase success at all costs, even if it means sacrificing our well-being. We've got a generation burning out and living only for ourselves, and it's a cry for change.

We're on a quest for meaning, but we don't know what that feels like or when we'll achieve it. We're scrolling, swiping, shopping – anything to numb that sense of emptiness – but it's all in vain. The real treasure isn't in the next binge-watch or online shopping spree, or even the next big paycheck; it's in the connection to our true God given purpose. We're standing at the crossroads of discontent and yearning. We've seen the impact on our mental health, and it's a sobering wake-up call. Society's prescription of "success at any cost" isn't cutting it.

I am not here to rain on your parade or shatter anyone's big dreams. I'm here to support and uplift those dreams. There is a secret to all of this, and it is available to every single individual. I'm here to discuss that the journey to purpose is simple and easy, and that our world has convoluted it into a money-making giant of an issue.

Now, let's take a moment to reflect on how we got here, where purpose has been reduced to a buzzword and a marketable product.

Historically, *purpose* was deeply ingrained in our culture, shaping our philosophies, religions, and literature. But over time, this profound personal quest got commodified. It turned into a brand, a trendy hashtag. An excuse for not being or doing what we were created to do because we were disconnected.

There's a whole industry out there with books, seminars, and online courses promising to reveal our purpose. A legion of so-called experts and coaches swear they've got the magic key to unlock our potential. This industry thrives on our collective quest for more. This is a huge issue and is making individuals profit in the name of coaching and helping, and as I stated earlier, it's adding to *their* bank account and isn't *truly* helping.

We've been so distracted by society's teachings that we have lost sight of the truth.

Our purpose is *within us*.

Each of us. This world and our busyness have pushed it and buried it deep within us. It's time to unearth it. To find it. To see the signs all around us, to follow our passions and listen to what is being spoken to us and over us. To become available to hear and to be led.

Here's the truth: I've been down this deep dark rabbit hole. I've chased purpose like a madman and lost myself in the process. A few times. As you have read, I've worn more hats than I care to admit and done even more in the name of finding that *more* – from a trained military sniper to a preacher, a personal trainer to a tattoo artist, and everything in between. And guess what? Despite all those different roles, the traditional pursuit of purpose always left me high and dry. I was busy. I was hustling. I was doing it exactly the way this world teaches, and it all led to my shipwreck.

So, why the hell is *purpose* such a hot topic? Why is it so alluring? Why are we collectively obsessed with this idea?

It's because that is what God created us for. It's the reason we are here. It's that longing for more that only His perfect plan can fill. Now, I know this can be a touchy subject and *lots* of people can and will argue this. Some will say God created you for *one* singular thing and it's up to us to find it. Some will say they don't want to be boxed in by God's plan because they want to have a choice. Well guess what… you can have both.

You do get to choose what path you take. You are doing it right now. The passions you have are from God. He knows the best plan for you, and He knows what will fill that void in your life and bring fulfillment. He knows exactly what choices you will make with your free will even before you make them, and He knows if and when you will surrender your life to His greater plan. We do not know what is best. His plan is the best plan, and it uses every ounce of passion and good desire that is within us. The choice this world is making is to ignore that and force our own way. Trust me, that's what I have done in multiple seasons of my life.

We're bombarded with stories of successful folks who seem to have it all figured out. They tell us that unless our lives look like theirs then we aren't living our purpose. Can *purpose* be neatly packaged and labeled like a store-bought product? Maybe it can. Maybe we are shopping and just looking in the wrong stores. We advertise *purpose* being sold here and the truth is it's all a façade. A counterfeit product being sold on the black market. An illusion of fulfillment. Now, we must figure out where to look.

What if your purpose isn't some fixed destination, but a constantly evolving journey? What if instead of a destination it's this very present moment? This very day? What if it's a deeply personal and fluid experience, not some one-size-fits-all job, hobby, or level of wealth? What if the quest for purpose isn't about finding answers but asking the right questions?

We get so wrapped up in the answers and the end goal that we don't see the journey and the beauty that is right here and now.

Your purpose is *now*.

This book is different. It's not about handing some pre-packaged "why" and pretending it'll fit everyone like a glove.

Because we don't need a "why" to have purpose, we need to have a *who* and understand *who* created us. We need to know *who* we are and what we were created for — our God-given purpose for this day.

The problem with mainstream self-help is that it lures most of us into a trap of overthinking, overanalyzing and over feeling. It feeds this idea that we must have all these moving pieces to truly be on the road to our dreams. That we need to have a grand, clear-cut plan to make it big enough to be fulfilled. And that's just plain wrong. Don't get me wrong, we have to *do,* but there is a simple step that must be taken before we hustle and grind.

Let me tell you something that those mainstream self-help gurus won't admit – life is messy, and purpose is often found in the mess. It's in the imperfections, the mistakes, the uncertainty. We don't need a perfectly polished "why" to live purposeful lives. You do not have to have your life all figured out. Ditch the idea that purpose only comes to the lucky, the rich or to the ones who hustle hard every single day. Instead, dive deep into the idea that purpose is, and has always been, *within us* and to find it we must be looking in the right place.

If you're tired of the same old self-help that's been regurgitated a million times, you're in the right place. This book is a breath of fresh air in a stagnant sea of mainstream messages. When we reach the end of our journey, you'll see that *purpose* isn't about digging up hidden truths, but unveiling our authentic selves.

Chapter 6: Real Is Rare

Let me ask you a question.

Who do you believe, deep down in your soul, that God will use?

The real you that He created – the one that was perfectly designed for greatness through a purpose that brings absolute joy and fulfillment through every flaw, mistake, and anything else you deem unworthy?

Or is he going to use the illusion of you that you show the world – the one that you hold a veil around to hide your ugly, to cover your mistakes and to be seen as someone who you really aren't?

This world is so full of fake; so full of the illusions of "authentic" people. Some will go hard and create a persona of ruthless toughness to hide the insecurities they really feel. Some will go soft to cover the pain deep within. Everywhere we look we see the illusion that people want us to see, the version of them that *they* believe is perfect and who they are supposed to be.

To answer my question, God is going to use the *you* that He created, and not this fake version you are showing the world or the model you truly believe with all that you are that you are supposed to be.

We create this fog, this illusion because we see ourselves the way the world does. The way the people around us do. We take on their beliefs about us as our own and begin to mold to that design. That is not the original blueprint. What causes us to build, grow, and change in this way? We believe what others are saying because of our flaws; because of our failures; because of the situations that hurt us and caused so much pain and hardship in life. We believe that God can't use that anymore.

I'm here to tell you that He can and He will. He is waiting for the real *you* to emerge. The *you* that looks at what He says about you and not what the world does. The *you* that is raw and real. The *you* that is willing to look deep within and say, "yes, I'm messed up. I made mistakes and I see it but *I* am not a mistake."

That is when God does His greatest work. Stop hiding the *you* that He wants to show the world. When you allow yourself to truly be yourself, the healing begins. The acceptance of yourself comes in abundance and the release of the things that don't serve you become effortless.

I found my purpose after my life completely went to the bottom of the ocean. I created a shipwreck of a life adorned with flowers and beauty. It was beautified destruction. I did not know who I was or what I wanted. It took me even lower than rock bottom on several occasions, but I ended up coming out of it on top of the mountain because it drove me to *truly* find myself and why I was here... my God-created purpose.

Purpose isn't about chasing some golden ticket to success or filling your life with fancy toys. It's not about wearing a shiny facade on social media while feeling empty inside. No, *purpose* is something deeper, grittier, and more genuine than that.

Purpose, as I've discovered, is about authenticity. It's about stripping away the masks we wear to fit into society's expectations and revealing our true selves. The *self* that God created. He knew what he was doing, so we shouldn't be hiding it. It's daring to be vulnerable, to embrace our flaws, and to connect with others on a raw, human level. To take risks and have faith. To be led first.

Purpose is about taking a step back from the relentless hustle culture and asking yourself, "What truly matters?" It's about finding meaning in the small moments, the quiet conversations, and the simple joys. It's realizing that life isn't a race; it's a journey, and every twist and turn is part of the adventure.

Purpose, for me, is about making a difference. It's about using my unique talents and passions to leave the world better than I found it. It's not about the size of a paycheck; it's about the impact we have on others' lives. The paychecks will come. The stuff will come. The happiness, comfort, joy, peace, and gratitude all come and bring more fulfillment than you could ever imagine.

The point of life is to embrace the messy, beautiful chaos that comes with it. It's about understanding that it's acceptable and human to stumble, to fall, and to get back up again. It's about learning from the mistakes and growing stronger with each challenge. Seeing the lessons and gifts within each struggle and hard time, not just getting back up as the same person with the same mindset, but improving and leveling up at every roadblock.

My intention is that this section makes you reflect on how you treat others and accept the mistakes that they've made. Think about times you were offended, hurt, or misled by someone and look at the big picture. Were they lost? Were they struggling?

Were they wandering and grasping at straws trying to find their own purpose?

My hope is that you do not take all hurt in your life personally, but rather you seek to see others as good and human. We have all been lost, and we are all working to be better and find the meaning of it all. Maybe we should give each other a bit more love, acceptance, and grace. Just maybe.

When I think about purpose, I see a path not defined by society's rules. It's a path unique to each of us, a journey of self-discovery, growth, and connection. It's about being unapologetically *me* and embracing the messy, imperfect, wonderful adventure of life.

Let's chat a bit about a few widespread misconceptions surrounding these ideas:

Purpose is found in your career. Yes, people are very successful and use their careers to bring true change in this world. However, it is not the career itself that is the achievement – it's how you use it. The *you* that is in the career, the hobby, or even the volunteer role is what transforms it into a catalyst. Whatever it is that you put your heart and mind into, *you* are the key to its fruition.

For example, becoming a lawyer is a career path. Choosing this path doesn't make it your purpose or a life well lived. You could use this path for illegal means or to help dangerous people for financial gain. On the flip side, you could use it to pour your heart into, truly help people in need, and make a difference in the lives of those who need it most. God only created you for one of those avenues and it's up to you to be willing to be led down the right path and resist man-made temptations.

Society feeds us this fantasy that once we pinpoint our career path we have found our true purpose for our life. With degree in hand, everything falls into place, and we live in eternal bliss. But guess what? That's not it. This is what causes us as a world to embody who we *think* we need to be to fit in.

Rooted in the "hustle and grind" culture are business people, coaches, entrepreneurs, and so many others. These are the people who yell and scream at you to rebel against the status quo, when they themselves fall in line behind everyone else in their arena. They are modeling their leadership and coaching after those that came before them – the exact maneuver they are advising you *not* to do – and becoming the flashy, wealthy public figure they think they should be now that they have that "career," life, or title.

Purpose isn't an endgame; it's a never-ending rollercoaster of a journey filled with love, acceptance, truth, peace, and most of all the *real* you. You can't have true love, peace, and acceptance for a person who doesn't really even exist.

Purpose is autonomous authenticity.

Throughout life, we grow, circumstances change, and priorities flip like pancakes. That "purpose" we thought we figured out a few years back might feel as distant as Pluto because the environment we are in changes. *We* are the constant. *We* are the purpose. The real *we*.

For years, I chased what I believed was my purpose, dipping my toes into various careers. I thought I had it all figured out, only to discover my purpose was not at all what I thought or imagined, and I was way off course.

This whole "endpoint" view of purpose? It's like being handed a platter of food and being told, "This is all you get for life, buddy." No wonder so many of us feel lost in a maze.

Here's another fun misconception: thinking that purpose must be grand, earth-shattering, and something that makes headlines.

We're bombarded with stories of folks who started world-changing charities, conquered towering mountains, or wrote New York Times bestsellers. While those feats are impressive, they aren't the only markers of purpose.

These accolades are the stories we see and tell ourselves we will never get to that point. It's not true. Life becomes grand when we finally find our footing on the path we were created to be on. Abundance and favor flow in ways we never imagined. So, the beginning may not be grand or earth-shattering, but I guarantee you the end fulfillment and legacy you were called to live will be.

We all will confront our purpose through a different lens. We have all been given different things that drive us and desires and passions that overwhelm us. Each of our stories will be unique, and if we stick to being our authentic selves then our stories will be rare enough for history to share.

Purpose can be found in everyday moments, fleeting acts of kindness, and the bonds we nurture. It doesn't always have to be in the spotlight; sometimes, it's the unsung hero in the background. Your purpose could be as simple as being a kickass parent, a dependable friend, or a thoughtful neighbor. It's about making a difference in our own way because we are each unique.

You are one of a kind, and there is no one else like you. God created you and gave you those passions, those desires, and you will be led to find the path to use them to the greatest extent you can.

So, why are we tangled up in these myths? Why do we see this obsession with purpose as some unmovable point or a grand slam achievement? It's our societal brainwashing; we've been conditioned to believe that our worth is tied to accomplishments and that it's all about actions, not our true essence. We're living in a world that worships the relentless hustle, making us think that without nonstop ambition, we're just lagging behind.

Living life with real authentic and genuine purpose colors the way we see the world. Rocking that purpose-driven mindset is like wearing shades that unveil opportunities and connections we never noticed before. We become pros at making deliberate decisions, more aware of the ripples we create in other people's lives, and start vibing with our values and dreams on a whole new level.

Think of it as seeing life through purpose-tinted glasses. Suddenly, the world looks different. We start spotting those moments that light us up, activities that bring us pure joy, and people who resonate with our energy. It's like a treasure hunt for meaning, with clues scattered all over. It becomes everything we see no matter which way we turn. It also shows us what doesn't fit. The fake. The illusion and the fog. We begin to see the entire picture and are able to see purpose with clarity and wisdom.

Now, before we go on to the rest of this book, let's talk about purpose as a divine design. Not everyone's on the same spiritual wavelength, and that is irrelevant. Whether we believe in a higher power, the cosmic flow, or the interconnectedness of all things, the idea of purpose as a divine intention can resonate with different viewpoints.

Before we even took our first breath, there was a design in place – a sacred blueprint for our lives. Call it destiny, fate, or whatever floats your boat, but the underlying basis is that there's a bigger purpose we might not fully understand that is intricately woven into our very existence.

Think of it like a jigsaw puzzle. Every piece represents an event, a choice, or an experience, all coming together to create a bigger, deeper picture. We might not see the whole image right away, and some pieces might seem insignificant or downright challenging, but each has its place in the grand scheme of things.

So, how in the world do we sync up with this sacred blueprint? How do we coincide with God's purpose – or whatever higher force or universal consciousness you connect with?

It starts with a change in perspective. Instead of seeing purpose as some prize you must chase down, view it as a treasure literally in your hands right now, waiting to be discovered and cherished. It's about the *now*, the present. It's less about achievement and more about transformation. It's about embracing roles and experiences that resonate with our divine intention. To take hold of this treasure means we have to release the person we thought we were and have fought so long and hard to keep even when it doesn't serve us any longer. After all of the roads I have taken to get here, I can see how it was all part of the plan. Every distinct time in my life shaped me, and all the pieces fit perfectly together when I look back and recognize the gifts of it all. As we will get into later, my story definitely didn't go the way I planned, but I can still look back and see how it all fit together and brought me to *this* perfect place.

As I stated, some might argue that surrendering to a divine plan feels like giving up control. After all, don't we all want to steer our own destiny? But here's the twist: embracing purpose like this isn't about losing control; it's about gaining true freedom. It's not about being lazy and just letting life happen either. It's being truly intentional with your life. It's about being aligned and so in tune with the divine that your life is being led to things you never imagined possible.

This is the sweet spot. This is the right place to be.

By acknowledging a purpose that transcends our personal, individual life, we can break free from the constant chase for recognition and external validation. It allows us to let go of the need to manufacture our purpose and focus on discovering and aligning with it instead. This kind of surrender fosters a deeper trust and belief. It's about having faith in a divine plan, even when we can't see the whole picture.

Seeing purpose as a divine design is just one perspective. It might not resonate with everyone, and that's okay. But what it highlights is that purpose isn't about our own work and plan; it's about embracing a bigger design that, even when it seems mysterious, can be trusted and embraced with all our hearts and will bring about the desires and passions in our hearts. Purpose flows with acceptance. God has a place specifically designed for me. God has a place specifically designed for *you*, and it's not a place where you are trying to be someone you aren't, or desperately trying to fit in. That isn't it. Release it and embrace who you truly are.

I embraced the ugly. The raw. The present. The day. The chaotic mess that was my life. The mistakes that made me believe I was a mistake. The thoughts and beliefs that drove me to paths to be accepted. I embraced *me*.

Real is rare.

Chapter 7: Led By Limiting Beliefs

Religion and the way we have twisted it up in places like churches have seriously messed with this world, leaving people on paths that suck the life out of them. It's like a heavy anchor dragging us back instead of moving forward. I can't speak for every belief or church out there, but from what I experienced growing up, the true message is buried under layers of B.S., rules, and fear mongering that make you feel worthless. To really get what God's about, we need to peel away that junk and dig into the truth.

Religion has turned into a breeding ground for a bunch of carefully directed guidelines and threats about eternal damnation. The true spiritual heart isn't about religion, it's about faith and love. It's about community. Now, I'm not here to trash religion entirely. I love my faith and God — but the only way I connected with a higher power was on my own personal journey, seeking comfort, guidance, and purpose while doing what I thought God was speaking to me in my very own, real, and crazy way.

I've learned that all the human-made religious stuff clouds your mind and takes away from true faith. So, what about these messed-up beliefs? They come in all sorts of flavors. It's the notion that there's only one way to find God, and everything else leads to doom. It's the fear of questioning or exploring other beliefs or even questioning how our texts are interpreted.

Let me be clear: these jaded beliefs, especially when they're harshly enforced by churches or leaders, have sent us down some messed-up roads. They bring fear and guilt, and stifle individuality. They crush your ability to love autonomously, show compassion, and grow personally. Living in that straitjacket means fewer chances to learn, expand, and find what works for you. It's a life with no room to breathe. There's no room to question, contest, and find God in your own personal way.

Now, at the core of all this mess is finding your purpose. You are here for a reason. You are here for total abundance and God made you with everything you need to live a life that is way beyond anything you could ever hope or imagine. God's already got a plan for you and will nudge you on the path to fulfill it.

In my life, I was lost in my own tangled mind. I couldn't see what was up as I was spinning through my own life, all the while being negatively influenced by the church. The God I was introduced to was battling the God that I wanted to believe in. I was overwhelmed by the standards I put on myself to be accepted and all that the world expected from me.

And yet, in the middle of my mental turmoil, I had a deep realization. I wasn't the one who found God; He created me and was whispering to me and guiding me back to Him the whole time. This realization caused a change in me; I stopped focusing on the external things and started focusing on peace and surrender.

With this new point of view, I set out on a journey that was guided by a higher purpose that was intricately woven into the fabric of reality. I stopped pushing to create my own purpose and started focusing on the desires and gifts inside of me. The ones God gave me to use for His ultimate purpose for my life. Knowing

I was a part of something bigger than myself gave me comfort and peace. In the end, my revelation showed me how complete surrender leads to freedom and can change everything.

A big part of my story was about the church and I also want to touch on limiting beliefs as a whole. These can come in all shapes and sizes, and get placed upon us in ways and circumstances we may not even be aware of. They could stem from parents never showing love or affection during childhood when our brains are sensitive to development and influence. They could result from a loved and respected figure telling us that we're annoying, fat, ugly, not good enough, not strong enough, not smart enough, not special enough, not worthy enough, not nice enough, not tall enough, not driven enough, not not not…

These words and beliefs of others, when told to us in vulnerable times or over the course of multiple occurrences, can and will sink deep within us and create limiting beliefs that we begin to accept as truth. These beliefs creep in from every situation in our past. These could be things we deem as normal, but in reality are completely inaccurate and subjective. They condition us to believe the only reality we have ever known is all we'll ever be. They construct our comfort zones. We may begin to push away anything that's different (sometimes this can mean "good") that comes into our life. We fight to stay in our dysfunction. We battle to stay within our chaos.

I grew up not believing in myself, which caused me to act in the ways explained in my story. This caused changes in my behavior and even the total lack of ownership or responsibility over my life and how I treated others. I was taking actions and making choices to show that I wasn't any of the things that I believed about myself, which caused me to force my own way. I was living a life to prove others wrong and when I failed miserably I proved them right; then I would set out on a path to do it all over again. This was the cycle of my destruction.

What you believe is what you receive.

For me, my core limiting belief was that if people knew the *real* me then they would reject me. This was not my actual belief. This is the point. This is what was *shown to me*, not what was actually in my heart. I believed that I had to be punished still, even though Jesus took it all for me. I believed that my life had to have this chaos within it in order for it to have meaning. I believed this so much that I created it. The mistakes I made were just symptoms of this belief.

We all have our go-to areas for sabotage and destruction, and they all come from the limiting beliefs that have been planted and watered within us. The more I kept my beliefs inside the worse it became. I was living life on a rollercoaster, and I was the operator. My shame and guilt grew and grew as my mistakes multiplied and all the while longing to be set free.

What would it take to get off this ride that was making me sick each and every single day? What was I afraid of? Facing the real me? Was I not cool enough, wise enough, good enough? Was it truly the rejection that I feared if the true me was revealed?

The truth is, it was a concoction of all the above.

Narcissist. I have been accused of this trait and called this name on numerous occasions, and yeah, it's true. The thing is, we all have these tendencies, and that's perfectly normal. This trait can also be expressed in ways that don't receive as much attention. Most would say that people who are all about themselves in grandiose and "positive" ways are narcissists. This is true, but the definition of *narcissism* is being all about oneself, positively or negatively.

"I am not good enough. I am causing this cycle. I am the cause of all this destruction. I am the reason these other people have terrible lives."

The list goes on. When you think you are so special or powerful that you are capable of being the cause of that much destruction, or to be the reason for all the bad things around you, then you are also exhibiting narcissistic behavior.

It's not all about you.

I did things to make people leave me because I wanted to give them a good reason to. I needed the blame to be on my action or behavior, not because of me, but because deep down I needed to confirm my belief that I just wasn't good enough.

Does that make sense?

It's so crazy because this type of separation usually frees people from their past, and I was using it to keep me in mine.

I am not my past.

Yes, I did those things, but they do not define me, and those actions are not my legacy. I had to come clean as I had tried on so many occasions before. I am not talking about coming clean to the world; I am talking about coming clean to myself. When I identified who I really was, who I have been because of the past hurts and beliefs that I have held onto, then I became a man who is content in himself and who doesn't need anyone to validate or approve him. I became a man that is ok with someone leaving or rejecting him because I know God created me to be right in this very place with who I have. Everyone plays a part. His plan is greater than anything I could have ever imagined.

You have to be honest with yourself, or nothing else can happen. It's ugly. It's hard. It's the worst, and it's the best thing you can possibly do for yourself. The truth does set you free and reveals your true self, your true flaws, and your true heart's character. It also reveals the past hurts, traumas, limiting beliefs, and all that you have allowed to define you for so long. All the things that you have allowed to be embedded in your life.

God loves you. He also loves *me*.

This is such a basic statement that carries the weight of the universe behind it. My limiting belief was that I had to earn His love. Even through everything I had endured growing up in the church, becoming a pastor, and through all of the lies, the hiding, and the cheating, I still looked for things in my life to blame my discontentment on. To blame why I wasn't where I believed I was supposed to be. I knew all the right words and cliché statements to make, but the truth is I didn't believe that God could love *me*. I didn't believe that He was sovereign enough to give me grace for my mistakes, but He could and would use them anyway.

I wanted perfection even through all my imperfection. I sought it, I expected it, I pushed things away, and even damaged myself more in the process. God had to be there. God *was* there in the midst of it all just calling me out from the depths of my own self-dug pit. Whispering so gently to just let it go.

I did.

I embraced this imperfectly perfect version of myself, and I still to this day look for the right ways to proceed. I also know that my God is for me, and He will always provide a way. I seek after the purpose He created me for and everything else will be and has been provided to me in every way.

Finding *my* faith has really changed how I see myself and my place in the world. It helped me understand that the way I've always seen myself as different from others isn't a flaw but a special part of who I am, made by God.

There have been many times of uncertainty and resistance throughout my life. I've wondered if being different was bad, especially when people close to me – even in church – didn't believe me or didn't like how I was different. Those closest to me constantly told me that my way wouldn't work or that I wouldn't amount to much, so I should just be "normal." Be mundane.

However, through it all, I've learned that my worth isn't based on what other people think; it's based on God's love for me, no matter what.

I found comfort in knowing that God's love never changes, even when I was going through hard times and no one seemed to be there for me – even times when people physically left me.

I am God's creation, so even though there were problems and questions along the way, my spiritual journey has helped me accept myself and have faith in myself. I stand here today as proof of how hope can change things. I know that my identity isn't based on what other people think of me, but on the love and purpose that my Creator gave me. We all have limiting beliefs. Yours may be so buried that you would deny that they even exist.

I challenge you to take a close look at why you do the things that you do.

Why do you react in ways that produce chaos and instability? Why do your feelings and assumptions always go to the negative? Why do you fight for things that have no place in your life and don't help the goals you say you have?

These beliefs that you hold dear could be about yourself or even others. When they go unacknowledged, they rule. There is a reason we act in the ways that we do and it is beneficial for everyone to uncover where these come from so that we can clear the way to our true selves. Releasing these beliefs frees us from the *self* that has been created and manipulated by actions against us in the past, or the past we are holding so tightly as ourselves. We are not those things.

Take the good from the past. Take the strength you have gained, but let go of the defensiveness you still hold. Find the gift. Uplift the individuality you have attained and let go of the belief that you must be different because you have been called so many names in the past. Love and cherish the heart of empathy that past disasters have created but let go of the belief that you need to always take care of others otherwise they will leave you.

We are unique and our stories shape us in such beautiful ways. It is up to each of us to dive in and recognize those ways. Keep what helps us and get rid of the things that don't. This is our life. Our past does not define us and is not our legacy. What we do from this moment forward can be the greatest purpose we have ever known.

Release what doesn't serve you anymore and make room for the new. The love. The abundance. The peace.

Chapter 8: In Your Corner

As I live my life, I strive to be a person who can bring God's love, power, and miracles back into this world for others to see who they really are in God. For me to get to this place took an extraordinary amount of courage, determination, and even more pain.

One of the pains that I clung to was that I was alone in my pit. Did I have people around me? Yes. Did they see my behavior and choose to not say anything? Yes. Did I reach out for help?

Nope.

In this section, I challenge and encourage you to get help. By doing so you are not weaker than, you are not less than; you are still the *you* that God created. Do not let this life fly by staying stuck in the same old behavior and cycles that you yourself are causing alone. I am speaking this from a very clear and painful experience. There are people in your life willing and able to show grace towards you no matter what.

I also advise you to not just grab any old friend to tell them your deepest, darkest secrets. These people must be your true "ride or dies." This circle is tiny – well, it should be. If it's not, then you are spreading your energy much too thin, and I challenge you to identify if any of those closest to you actually know the real *you*.

Your inner circle are the ones who know where the bodies are hidden and won't rat you out (kidding). These people are the ones you trust with your life, your secrets, your feelings, your regrets, your biggest faiths, and fears. These are the people who stick by your side even when you make mistakes or if they don't agree with a choice you have made. Find those people if you don't have them. Everyone needs people in their corner. *Real* people. Not ones who look good on social media. Not superficial, "we are friends on Facebook" friends.

These are the people who know it all.

I had a dear friend and mentor; Mr. Lou. Mr. Lou was the epitome of gratitude, fortitude, life, and strength. His motto was to "live full and die empty," and he taught me so much more than I could ever express. He was my instructor, my friend, and always showed me immense grace. Mr. Lou is a perfect example for this section because he was always in my corner, even literally because he was my martial arts instructor and was in my corner when I fought.

The next point goes out to these inner circle members: be real. No matter how you feel about your own life and purpose, you are a member of someone else's inner circle and need to be ready and available to be called on. Be able to be confided in. Be trustworthy. Remember: real is rare. Be rare for your people. It is your responsibility to call each other out.

Your job in this position is to have integrity, to be honest and loyal. If you do not speak up regarding the negative behavior someone confides in you, then you are just enabling, and you don't deserve to be in that inner circle. You also don't get to hold this position if you aren't trustworthy enough with all of the facts – seek the facts, challenge perspectives, and help someone see the whole picture and how God sees them.

Want to know who your true friends are? They are the ones who speak the truth in good times and bad, when you want to hear it – and especially when you don't. They are the ones who see the toxic cycle of old and love you enough to not allow it to continue. They are the ones who see through the feelings and see the big picture. There will be times when an inner shift happens with someone or circumstances change, and you have to trust and stay loyal to your people even if you don't see things their way. Believe in them and believe the best for them even if you don't agree or they are heading down the "same road." It may not be the same road in the long run, and they need you to stand by them no matter what.

In our lives we are faced with challenges that we have not encountered before, and any successful person will tell you that's why you surround yourself in your larger circle with people who have faced those challenges or built the dream you are trying to accomplish already. However, this circle of mentors, motivators, and idols can change and fluctuate depending on your goals and priorities at that time. This circle can be made up of those going on the same journey as you or even coaches or counselors.

Participating in counseling is *not* a sign of anything except wisdom and self reflection. There is a stigma around attending counseling (therapy) – especially for men – that is unnecessary and plaguing our society. I recommend counseling even if you don't believe that you have any issues. It's a great way to avoid preventable challenges in the first place; to tackle things before they even come up. This is also a great place to target those limiting beliefs and find out where they come from. The only issue you can potentially have with counseling is *you*. Yes, you read that right.

You.

Counseling is solely dependent on *you* wanting to be there — on you being willing, open, and able to tell the whole truth, nothing but the truth, and all the ugliness of *you*. If you cannot do that then counseling is a waste of time and money. If you go into therapy to blame others and avoid your own behavior, then your counselor gets just one side of the story and will side and agree with you. This is not helping you get better. By doing this, you are leading them to affirm behavior from the story given, which is going to be way off from reality. Your counselor is not there to diagnose or help anybody else, just *you*. They are not even interested in other people's behavior, just *yours*. Be open and refrain from responding defensively. Be open to hearing the truth or another view, and seek out opportunities for you to be *wrong* — it means you are on your way to change.

I want so desperately for you to be unstuck and living with freedom and abundance. So, if you are looking to dive deep within the one and only *you* and truly make changes, then go do the work.

Now, coaches. Ah, coaches. Yes, this is venturing into the self-help arena.

Not all coaches are scams. Not all coaches are driven by money, and there are some incredible paid mentors out there who operate to serve and help those they are entrusted to guide. The most important advice I can give you, gleaned from my own experience, is to get to know your coach on a personal level before paying them to help shape your mindset and your direction. Many times this looks like asking for a trial period within reason to make sure you feel your coach has your best interests at heart, and will listen to your drive to find your purpose and build a genuine legacy. If you feel an advertised "coach" is not authentic or does not act the same out of the spotlight as they do on a stage, then run for the hills. Keep your money until you find the right person for *you*, and ensure you are mentally and emotionally in a place to turn your life upside down. You are trusting your life and mindset in the hands of a person you genuinely trust and respect. Do not pay for a fix – invest in your guided growth.

As we discussed earlier – real is rare, and it takes some work and effort to uncover the people who God means for you to have in your life – whether for a lifetime or a season. Choosing someone you trust enough to coach you is just like being in a relationship. Both parties must put in 100%. It's not 50/50 – it's 100/100.

In my lifetime I have had multiple coaches and counselors. In the early stages these relationships didn't work out because I wasn't ready and willing to be completely honest and vulnerable. Once I was in a place to see and hear a contradicting perspective, I began to seek out all the help I could get.

On one occasion I had a counselor that began to reinforce my limiting beliefs during the time we worked together. I had already paid upfront for the work to be done because I was all in and excited to roll. In my very first session with this individual, I knew we were not going to work. I had heard raving reviews from multiple people about this counselor, but the truth was, we couldn't have been more at odds. I was open to hearing about where I could improve and where I truly was in this journey, but all this person could do was point out the things in my life that they did not agree with. They could not move past the fact that I had tattoos and piercings and that I was also a pastor. I was there to do work and they were unable to see past their prejudices and beliefs. I caught the damage before his opinions could poison my mind and we parted ways at a loss for me.

Be careful who you trust to influence your mind. Not everyone in your circle is in your corner. You deserve effort being put into you. You are worth it. Just because one mentor or guide didn't work out, doesn't mean you put up your walls and defenses and claim that you are hopeless. Be open and positive to someone arriving in your life precisely when God intends them to. Uplift your energy and you will attract who and what you are looking for.

After my unfortunate counselor encounter I did some research and found someone I believed would fit perfectly. We did. This counselor was by my side through some pretty major events as well as even greater discoveries about myself. I am truly grateful and forever will be to this individual and the impact that they had on my life.

You need to be in your own corner. For many, this could very well mean going against many people in your life who are important to you. I have close people in my life who wanted and believed all I was meant for was a 9-5 job and a normal life. I knew there was more in store for me. It caused friction in my relationships with those individuals and left many topics of conversation off the table to avoid conflict and arguments. You must be rooting and fighting for yourself against anything and anyone who says or believes differently. You must believe that you are better than what your lifetime narrative has painted you as, and more valuable than the comfort zone you have been stuck in. You need to be your biggest fan. I don't mean that in an egotistical, narcissistic way – I mean, love yourself. Believe in the great things that you possess because God put them there. Spend the time to love yourself like your life depends on it and show yourself what you truly deserve.

The very beginning of this process is getting to know your Creator – whatever that means to you. To know the divine is to know yourself. To see the beauty in nature is to see the heart of the artist who created it. Your Creator has some pretty incredible things to say about you, and you need to hear it. You need to let it soak in and allow it to become your beliefs and even your inherent emotions.

There are so many ways to dive into loving yourself. My suggestion: read. Get that knowledge within you and borrow other people's mantras and helpful tricks to jumpstart your life. It's okay to steal from other people's ideas to better your thoughts about yourself. That's literally why these types of books are written. Begin to meditate and look and feel within. When I began to meditate it was awful. I sucked at it. I couldn't sit still and I couldn't stop my brain from wandering. Now, meditation is a huge part of my life, routine, and healing. You cannot control your mind until you first train it to become still.

Take the knowledge that you have gained from reading the thoughts and motivations of others and meditate. Go into the stillness. Get to know yourself. Love yourself by picturing your ideal self living with purpose and reflecting on who you need to become to make that happen.

Use your inner circle. These are the people who know you best and want to be there to help and support you in every way. If you don't have an inner circle then put yourself in places where you are surrounded by people who have things in common, and you will find your people.

When all else fails – know that I am in your corner. My passion is to help others, to truly partner, and to create lasting change. My own life went through hell to help others avoid it, and that for me makes it all worth it. You are worth it. Your life is worth it, and the work is worth it. God has big plans for you, and no matter where you are and what you are facing, God has this.

And in this corner: God.

The divine is here and working in and through you for all things. We are powerful creators, and yet most of us walk around this earth like we are nothing. No wonder what we attract and what comes our way is exactly what we believed, felt, and thought. Yes, we are *that* powerful and it can be used to bring abundance, freedom, unity, power, wholeness, joy, and love… *or* it can bring all the negativity your heart and mind are stuck on. It's your choice.

God says so many things about you and none of them are bad, my friend. We *must* find out who God created us to be, because that is who He sees us as in this very moment.

You see, He sees us as what we will be, and we must do the same. You already have everything you need. Know it. Feel it. What we think and feel is what we bring into our lives. I was driven by my purpose, so the things I felt and thought about came to pass. Previously, I was so focused on my limiting beliefs and the fight of who I believed I was that my beliefs took shape and brought the circumstances that I focused on. If you believe in things enough and even speak them out loud you will see them happen. Good or bad. Yes, you can say that I was the one who took the action, but look at the story and see the many things that came my way. I didn't force them to come my way, they just showed up. They came because of my negative beliefs which became negative thoughts, and then negative feelings, and then tangible negatives.

You are powerful – so much more than you realize. What you spend your time thinking about and putting feeling behind *will* happen... good or bad.

I want you to unlock your true power for the best life you could ever imagine. When I say I am in your corner, I mean it. All of these circumstances have perfectly shaped my life to be driven by a true purpose and a passion to help others do the same. Through coaching of my own I am able to help others uncover their limiting beliefs and move towards and build incredible lives of purpose here and now.

Chapter 9: Clarity Within

As you can see, the story of my life began quite some time ago and has lots of twists and turns. I struggled for a long time. The visual struggles are obvious – the things that came to pass because of my actions. But those actions were just the symptoms of a much deeper struggle; a thorn that would not leave me. This thorn has no name, just as Paul in the Bible talks about his thorn without revealing the issue. The things you see in this story can be the flowers or even the outlying thorns, but they are not the one true thorn for everyone. I focused on identifying my thorn, searching for *more*, and trying to reason and explain it all. I was attempting to find the smoking gun that could be eliminated to give me freedom.

Throughout my story I was constantly changing. I was working by my own strength, and I felt alone in that work, alone in my faith and in my belief for greater things. My hope was (and still is) great, and my faith was even greater. I believed so much in my God and His love, power, and grace, that I would do whatever I felt like doing to put Him to the test. What transpired during the hardships of my life was a result of my own actions – nothing that God inflicted on me. My choices and subsequent tragedies were derived from my strength and my desire for greatness, my drive toward my purpose in life, not His.

At one point, all that I had done in my life had fallen squarely on my shoulders, and I accept it now willingly because I see it so clearly. I see the cycle within myself.

Did I continue to do the work? Yes!

Did I stay true to my word? Yes!

Was it just a little too late for the marriage? Probably.

Was it like trying to patch the Titanic with bubble gum and duct tape? Yup.

I did everything I could. I gave it all that I had. I surrendered to everything.

Having to deal with the truth of my situation at the time required me to be alone. I realized at that moment that I had the power to make my own life, and it was my obligation and part of my healing to do it on my own, with God by my side, free from any and all influences of other people and any of my prior commitments based on a lie. I needed a clean slate. So I started over..

Now, marriage is a distant thought for me, a memory. What seems like a lifetime ago. Before it ended abruptly, things had been going so well. I was staying true to my word and putting in the work every single day to make it work and to be the best that I could be. There had been so much damage done that the inevitable happened – chaos.

The marriage was working and we had even made plans to move halfway across the country to join some other family members and have a fresh start to life. The week before the move I was triggered by an event that I remember so clearly to this day. My friend, a leader, a pillar of humanity, grace, and strength, passed away. Mr. Lou. He lived a full life and died empty. You see, my acts of betrayal had put me into a hole. A spot where I was disconnected from the world because of my actions to ensure I stayed in my lane. This disconnect kept me from friends and family, and when I was told about Mr. Lou, it was a couple months after it happened. My past behavior blocked me from the people I needed the most and even kept me from being there for the people I always vowed to show up for. I had failed Mr. Lou. This brought so many emotions into my life, and I fell into a dark place. This dark place gave way to the end of myself which is exactly where I needed to be. I still moved my family all together, but within a month I was out of our new house and on my own.

When you go searching for something, good or bad, you will find it. It's ugly, it's beautiful, it's terrifying, and it's freeing. What I found in my search was my struggle. What I found was devastating. What I found was clarity.

What I found was *purpose*.

My struggles have molded my life in ways I never would've imagined or planned. Since the beginning I've believed in something bigger, call it "God" or whatever you want, and I know it's got a grander vision for us than we can fathom. It takes the worst parts of us and turns them into something glorious. I've learned that the more I try to take control, the more I lose it. I've realized that I will continue to be molded until I realize that what He is trying to shape me into is something much more incredible that I ever could have crafted on my own.

I am confident in the interwovenness of my life, my faith, and purposes I'm yet to discover. My faith is unwavering, and my hope is solid as a rock. What makes me most proud is sticking to my beliefs, even when other people doubted me or said terrible things about me. Even when things got hard and people looked the other way (or physically left me) I knew that God was on my side and leading me forward. It gave me strength.

Despite those closest to me doubting and criticizing me, I'm proud of how determined I am to make the world a better place.

This book is all about laying the groundwork, the basics of human existence: faith, and love. Our world has strayed so damn far. We've lost sight of our identity in the One who created us all.

The journal, this book, is not meant to be a pity "poor me" party. I am not the victim nor am I trying to sway the story to shine light on myself. I desire for it to illuminate the darkness in others because I don't believe that I am alone. I am not the only one who is struggling with my God-given purpose, and trying to create it on my own – trying to find where I belong and who I really am.

Please do not get caught up in exactly what I did. See through it. See behind it and beside it. This is why Paul's thorn in the Bible is never identified – so all can feel and see themselves within the story.

See yourself within this story.

I'm penning this to share my journey, to throw my story out there – the highs, the lows, and the moments that spun me sideways. This journey isn't over, but it's led me to this place, a place of clarity and simplicity in the midst of all the chaos. Clarity is the simplicity hidden beneath the noise we create and let into our lives. To find that clarity, we've got to blow away the fog we've allowed to linger, the smoke and mirrors that give us a false sense of change and progress. My prayer is that my words strike a chord deep within you. I hope that my faith sparks a sense of peace, even an "aha" moment of the potential in your life and our world. We've shouldered enough, and it's time to strip things back to the essentials and reclaim our lives meant to be filled with joy, basking in the abundance that the divine has promised us right here on this earth.

I've been through countless phases and emotions on this journey, and I can tell you one thing for certain – I am damn well worthy. Like I've shared, it wasn't always like this. It didn't start this way. There were times when I'd heap all the blame on myself, drowning in shame and feeling unworthy of anyone's love and affection, and taking action to sabotage myself.

I couldn't believe that God could truly love me. Sure, I knew He could and did, but I couldn't believe it for myself – only for others.

My faith in a better life, a life worth living, was twisted by what I was taught and what I believed, even about myself back in those dark times. The darkest hours of our lives are the ones that bring the most brilliant light into the world. Life is about surrendering to a plan and purpose that isn't of our own making but is guided by the love and grace of the one true God.

My struggles and my journey created such chaos and destruction. Once the dust settled, I still pursued the work. I continue to discover my purpose, but with an ambition and drive that was unlike anything before.

My story created a clarity that I had never experienced before. It removed all the extra stuff. All the B.S. that clouds us as people and a modern culture.

I want to address some topics.

I want to start by saying that I am not one of those coaches claiming to offer you "self-help." I am not here to manipulate, or even deceive you to go down the wrong path just to make a few bucks. I am not here to make you anxious and miserable with vague words and lectures on your "why" that usually litter pages of books on *purpose*. That is not a cookie-cutter, one-size-fits-all approach to finding a so-called "why" in life. You've seen it, I've seen it – a never-ending parade of gurus and life coaches pushing their magic formulas to discover our *purpose*. They make it sound like once we find our "why," everything falls into place, and we'll live happily ever after.

I want to advocate for you to break free from those old-school beliefs that have been holding you back. I want you to rediscover the heart of spirituality. I want to help you get to know the intricacies of love and purpose.

It's time to step into our true purpose and let God guide us. This is the way to find real fulfillment, to live in tune with the divine plan, and create a world where love and purpose rule. Purpose is all about your connectedness to yourself. Within that connectedness is the divine.

In this age, we have created a world of busy-ness. We have created a world of illusion. We do the bare minimum or even "join" events and movements to relieve some tension and pressure on ourselves, but no work and no change is actually being done.

We are lost.

I see the world in a different way now. These battles that I've faced are what I see in so many people around me and in world leaders. They're caught in similar battles, driven by desires for power, love, money, and possessions. They occasionally justify themselves by tossing a bone to charity or performing a good deed for the year. As a whole our hearts are lost. We've lost sight of what it means to genuinely help others. Instead, we are merely creating the illusion of progress, coaching, and unity.

I now have the unique ability to make things very simple. To see the root to truly be able to fix the problems. When war and chaos are the epitome of your world for so long, then the bullets stop flying and your own self-destruction ceases, you can see the world for the beauty it truly possesses and acknowledge the simplistic details behind and under the complicated.

When did we add so much extra to our lives and beliefs? Why did we create a world where we fight and argue around small details that really don't matter?

The main thing is that the details can be created in your own life, but not as uniform laws for everyone to abide by.

Your purpose is rooted in accepting and loving others, even if you are not in agreement with the details they chose to add to their life. Respect them because they are loved by God just as you are.

Grace.

What I see is people lost in themselves. Grasping at anything, everything, and anyone to find their identity. It is not shameful or wrong to identify traits in other people and then take them and make your own, or even intentionally omit them.

I like how this person does this, or how this person acts toward their spouse. I hate how this person lies or isn't genuine.

To identify behaviors and traits to create and be the best version of yourself is exactly what we should be doing: striving to be better every single day to become who we truly were created to be.

The truth is that this world takes a look at a person and immediately says within themselves, "I want to be *that* person." Not, "I want to take this particular thing," but to actually *become* that person. I have witnessed this on so many levels, from the church world, to the coaching world, and everywhere in between.

We are not meant to worship a person. We are not supposed to desire to *become* that person. We have all done this at some point, and there is probably that desire within you about someone you have encountered or admired even to this day.

Churchgoers often worship the pastor – the person. The pastor even provides avenues for praise and adoration, disguising it by slapping Jesus' name on it. Coaches use the key phrases like, "I am trying to help as many people as I can," meanwhile charging a ton of money for *just* enough advice to keep you happily complacent. If they truly were to help you, you would not need them anymore and they would lose that admiration... and revenue. They are not helping or bringing change – just the illusion of change. The illusion of help.

"Who you are isn't working. Be like me... strive to be me... and you too can be as happy as I appear."

This illusion has blinded our world.

Clarity can see the motives through the fog of the illusion. This illusion includes the people we have put in prominent places, and the *actual* value they are bringing (or the illusion that is being spun.)

The self-help scene is flooded with folks claiming to have all the answers, swearing they'll revolutionize your life if you just follow their magic recipe, while ensuring that the greater good is at the forefront of their campaign. The people in positions of power and influence that are supposed to be making the biggest large-scale changes are hurting us the most. Their doctrines or agendas, fuel hate, division, poverty, and so much more. We have lost our sight. We have lost our leaders. We have lost our integrity. The people in power who are supposed to be showing us the love of God within our churches have caused division through details that don't matter.

Eat this, don't eat that. Worship here, but not there. Tithe this amount. You're allowed to say this, and definitely don't do that. You're not allowed to love this person or look this way.

How did all this get tied to God?

When will we get back to the truth and what is truly right? When will we learn to forego the distractions and focus on what actually matters; "keep the main thing the *main thing*?"

The real guidance we are yearning for comes from a place of humility. It comes from looking beyond our human selves, whether to God, a higher power, or a deeper purpose. I stand firm in my faith, and I believe that God is the way back to save our world.

Where has God gone?

We have forced Him out. Pushed Him away. Ignored His guidance and leadership. We have formed countless new religions because the existing ones don't fit our narrative or how we want to live.

Last time I checked, God did not intend for us to cherry pick his Word.

We have created this current world by any means necessary – lies, dishonesty and manipulation. By justifying our actions when we know the truth.

When will love and freedom be revealed again?

Who will take that stand?

Where do we go?

Is this the world we really want?

Is this the world we are proud of? Or the one that leaves a legacy worthy for our children?

We complain and complain about the land that we live in. The people in power. The decisions being made. Limiting beliefs in our lives hold us in a stronghold. A stuck place. When the collective is lost and succumbing to those stuck places then the consequences multiply. Our comfort zone as individuals is stuck within our own chaos because it's all we know. As a nation, that comfort zone becomes our dysfunction. Our lies. We complain about this place and say we don't enjoy it (and we don't), but we always fight to stay in it because what *could be* may be so much scarier. We crave chaos because it's comfortable. We complain and argue about where we are as a nation or a world but do nothing to change it. Change is hard and scary, and we don't know what that change will feel like, so we build the walls around our cozy chaos even higher.

What are you fighting to hold on to?

Change, or to reinforce your certainty within uncertainty?

When we take sides and proclaim we are right, are we any better than those leading the way to this stuck place?

To truly choose a leader now, we need people who have clarity and wisdom. We need people of integrity who fight for the greater good and to nudge us out of this rock and a hard place. We need leaders who don't take sides but look for where love and unity can bring us back together.

That is worth fighting for. True change and not just the illusion.

You are on this earth for a specific reason. The Creator of all has made you. Not just for a toy to move around and play make-believe. But to bring love, change, and his power into your world.

Do you command these things in your life?

So many of us are doing whatever we want to do to find fulfillment — we are trying to force an abundant life while having a sneaking suspicion it can only be found within the purpose we were created for. I know this very topic turns people off because they want to be in control of their destiny and live their own lives. I have heard it all, and that is where I feel many are mistaken.

God put every desire inside of you. Your dreams and interests are what make you, *you*. The *you* that you are trying to be. It comes from Him. Aligning those desires with the divine, with the Creator, unlocks everything you could have ever hoped for or dreamed of and even more. What you are chasing now will not even scratch the surface of what God's purpose is for you. You may achieve wealth and influence, but that does not equate to *purpose*. I see so many people using that influence to take sides and post their monumental achievements on social media in ways that communicate nothing but ego and selfishness.

I choose to be driven by purpose. His purpose for why He created *me*. I choose to be driven to speak these words. To bring power, love, and miracles back into this land that I love – this world that He created. To bring true change, not just the illusion, not just the keywords to act the part.

Imagine what this world would look like if we all took this to heart and believed in this change.

Our Western culture has this knack for painting success within these flashy colors, like it's a game for lions and wolves – the cutthroat bunch who'd step on anyone's toes to get ahead.

What if culture has got it all twisted?

What this world truly needs are folks who are willing to be sheep. Yes, you heard me right – sheep. I'm not directing you to follow the herd blindly; I'm talking about another kind of sheep. The kind that listens to a higher calling, rooted in faith and purpose. Acting as a sheep is about being in sync with the divine, willing to be led with a greater power, and seeking that guidance *before* charging ahead.

In a world screaming for us to be lions and wolves, those who choose to be sheep are often seen as weak or naive. But let me tell you, being a sheep in this sense takes real guts. It's about letting go of your own ego and trusting there's a bigger plan at work. It's not about blindly following anyone. It's about aligning with something deeper and letting it steer your ship.

So, let's talk about this.

Over my 40 years of life, I have heard just about every coaching reference involving animals that exists. There is one for every aspect of life or hobby.

If you've never encountered this, the idea takes an animal reference and tells us to take on those primal qualities of that beast. Be ferocious. Be cunning, fast, smart, hard, a fighter, a loner only relying on yourself. Get it? (I am in no way trying to call out any particular coaching group or mastermind).

In order to be any of those king or queen animals – ferocious fighters and people who know what they want and go after it with all they have – you have first to be a sheep. In these coaching talks, you will never hear the leaders telling their groups to go become sheep. *Why?*

It is because they only see the negative connotations of that idea, or even twist the positive animal attributes into bad things to fit a point they are trying to make. They imply sheep are followers and they go where the flock goes. They go exactly where the leader tells them to go because they can't defend themselves. They need others. They need protection. They are weak and they know it. They accept that their life is safer and more comfortable in someone else's hands. They have to trust someone else because they know that they themselves are not enough and can only go so far.

Raise your hand if you want to be a sheep.

Yeah, I didn't think so.

So, here is the twist and where I bring it back to some of my earlier points. I am not talking about wandering through this life as a sheep. We have so many sheep in this world. Weak and gullible. Following the newest trend, the newest coach…. *wait… but they tell us not to be a sheep… isn't that what we are doing by following them and joining their group… erm… flock?*

Weird.

I'm confused…. you told me I need to be a sheep?!

Yes, I did.

In your home. In your quiet place.

Be the sheep to the one Shepard — the God who created you for a specific purpose. Know that you alone are not enough on your own to do what he created you to do. You must follow Him. You must trust in Him. He leads.

I became that sheep during my time of darkness. I needed guidance deciding where to spend my days, spend my energy, and take action on what battles to engage in. I needed confirmation that would give me the strength to do so. I knew he would defend me and protect me. I knew he would fight for me and alongside me. I knew I was weak. I knew my life was in his hands, and I put my faith in him as a sheep to the Shepherd.

When you do this, He will always answer. He will lead. He will empower you to go from the surrendering sheep to the fighting predator. and becoming a leader for what is right.

The only way to fight in this life, the only way to become who you need to become, is first to be that sheep humbled by God's grace and strengthened by his power and love. *Driven by His purpose.*

Are you available for God to do His work? Are you open to being used by him?

Is your life filled with *stuff* to just be busy, not for any real purpose or true change?

What space can God take up? What places have you given him to fill?

What I am speaking about at this point is bringing true God-given change to your world. Then, our world. Most will probably say it's not possible. I disagree. With God, all things are possible. It just takes a spark.

Are you believing and dreaming big enough?

What are you waiting on God for? Do you really believe he can do it?

What have you given to him? What are you living for?

The most important things to us will appear in our daily routines and habits. What do yours show?

Are you solely focused on being the ferocious animal, taking this life on yourself? In your own strength? That will only get you so far, and it won't be fulfilling. Let the first 33 years of my life be an example to you. Let go of trying to do it yourself.

Are you overwhelmed with just surviving? Just making it through the day? Staying the sheep or living life in the façade of a victorious animal and not living with intention?

I faced a choice not that long ago.

As I mentioned, back in 2010, God promised to bring me to a place of influence. I heard His voice as clear as watching a sunset. I envisioned a platform that I was created specifically for. One that would come with the desires that were within my heart, aligning my desires with the divine to bring true change.

I did a lot of things after that promise. Things that tried to bring the promise to pass on my own and in my own power. Things that took me into a deep hole because I thought it was too late and I could never be used by God again.

It took me a long time to get out of that mess within my heart and head.

In 2023, God spoke again. He told me to be available. He told me to step away from my job and give that space to him. In the year prior, I had done a lot of things from coaching, as well as modeling and acting; trying to find my purpose in life – to create that platform He promised me in the way that I assumed he would provide it. Nothing had worked.

I was pushing in my own strength yet again and the time wasn't right. God told me to step aside. Give Him room and be available.

That's when the hard part started.

I had to wait… again.

The idea of a book was in my heart. I wrote it in my notes on my phone, and that's where it lived until June of 2023. During this time of waiting I felt something stir in my heart that my words were about ready to come out – on paper and into the world. As the book began to take shape, I revisited my longtime desire to become a speaker. I had created videos to bring the message I felt in my heart at the time, and I felt it in my bones that a physical book was where my message was supposed to go. I felt the alignment that I had been once again trying to force God's platform, but not actually listening to Him.

My book was to be filled with my thoughts that I believed God had given me. Thoughts that seemed different from others, but maybe just thoughts that were't shared as vocally. Perhaps not a new story or new ideas but different characters – a different view and angle. They needed to be shared. They needed to be in a package. Alltogether as one. I had to step up and be the change.

That change looked very different from society's version of "progress." The busyness of life opens multiple doors of opportunity for change, but it's in the stillness that we are shown our assignment that leads to our legacy and purpose.

Not every opportunity is your assignment.

I knew that while this book was being called to be written, the busyness needed to take a back seat.

In my journey I have had some pretty amazing realizations and in reality, they seem so insignificant and even backwards of what I felt like the goals were. That is what makes them so unique. I've learned that the stillness in life is required to see the real *you*. To see the real God. To see the divine working in and through you.

To recap and continue the story; God made me a promise long ago and filled me with great expectations and even bigger faith. The journey that I have unveiled to you is what happened since that promise – me trying with all that I had to bring that promise to fruition. Well friends, if God made the promise to you then it's His job to bring it. Get out of the way.

That is exactly what I *finally* did.

Chapter 10: Where Can We Go From Here?

When God spoke to me in a very clear way, I saw that I was falling back into my busyness and doing so many things that were not in alignment with the greater plan that my life was created for. I knew exactly what I needed to do.

Quit.

You heard me right. I had to stop the coaching I was doing. I had to put aside the modeling and acting career that I was pursuing. I had to quit my job.

Seems extreme, I know.

Now, before you slam this book shut, I am *not* advocating for you to quit the only source of income that you have. I am telling you that this was how much faith God put inside of *me* and I knew this was the route I had to take.

So, I did.

The message was so clear. The divine was asking me if I was even *available* to be used. Was I available to be sent out on the greater life that I was literally created to live?

Think of your calling like running into a great friend you had growing up who you haven't seen in years. Picture that you had lost touch somewhere along the way, but this person is one of those friendships that you just pick right back up where you left off. Your relationship doesn't even skip a beat. Well, this friend wants to continue the reminiscing and asks you to do lunch, so you check your calendar.... *full.*

Are you actually available or is your calendar packed so that you feel like you can't do anything extra?

Do you have any *room* for the divine to move in and through you?

Of course, in my brain I believed that I would take this massive step of faith and God would instantly bless me with a lotto jackpot and millions of dollars. It didn't quite go down like that. Immediately after taking this leap, I felt free. I felt like I was exactly where I was supposed to be and I didn't want to waste any time – I wanted to get after my purpose.

Hmmm…that sounds a lot like the "hustle and grind" culture we talked about earlier…

Exactly. Here is where my story illustrates this point in a big way. What was I supposed to be hustling after and grinding towards?

Exactly. I had *no* idea.

God was calling me to rest. To wait. I don't know about you, but these are probably the two most hated words in my vocabulary, and especially when they are spoken *to* me. That is not what I wanted to do and not what I expected at all.

So, there I was, no job, no income, and sitting around just waiting and resting in the promise that God had spoken over my life.

It's an incredible thing that we, as humans, can create busyness out of absolutely nothing. This is the place I found myself in. As I discussed before, filling our lives with *stuff*, with busy calendars, just keeps us in a fog. No matter if it's a day-today work hustle and bustle, HOA or PTA meetings, coaching, volunteering – whatever it may be – we find a way to stay occupied.

In my case I created a day filled with walking my dog, working out, planning my meals to stay in competitive shape, and finding other various activities to stay engaged. Even during these seemingly harmless activities I was not getting it. I am so grateful that His guidance was still there, showing me the way. I knew what I had to do.

I had to just *stop*. I had to wait. I had to move forward with purposeful intention to listen and to become available. I had to freeze and remain in the exact same position I had put myself in when I quit my job. I had to stay there. I had to listen and discover what greater things God had in store.

Creating a life of rest, of intentional waiting, is probably the most difficult endeavor we could ever embark on. It seems so easy, so unmonumental. I can tell you from personal experience that it sucks. I am an achiever. I go all in and all for the things I want to accomplish. The difference is that in those arenas, you are doing, moving, and achieving with tangible ways to see the progress.

So, I dove into deliberately doing *nothing* with all my power. I jumped in to surrendering with all of my strength. I moved to sit in the stillness with every muscle I had. I wrestled for clarity in every ounce of patience I possessed. I fought for freedom in every fleeting thought of fear that came my way. I grasped for gratitude with every negative naysayer or even old limiting belief within myself. I was fighting to rest. I was working to wait. I was becoming beyond myself and above anything I could have ever hoped or imagined. I was new.

This was not an easy, quick fix. Challenges came my way. People were against me at every turn and even I was too much of the time. Money became scarce and homelessness was on the horizon.

As my middle son would say, *"It's better this way."* He was right and I knew exactly what he meant. It *had* to be this way. It *had* to be where people saw it. It *had* to be so bad that those I was attached to had to see and even believe how stupid I was being. It *had* to come to a point where I was borrowing money to barely make deadlines, and where I couldn't afford the things that I was supposed to be responsible for.

This was an area I struggled big time. I didn't want others to be affected by my decisions and I hoped so much for God to allow me that courtesy. He didn't and for a good reason. It brought the renown of my "craziness." My "stupidity." My "selfishness." My "narcissism." Just "Brandon being the same 'ole Brandon." My downright "irresponsible behavior" that has been accused of "causing trauma for my kids from day one," and everything else people said about me.

These thoughts, these criticisms, came from the people closest to me; from the people who said they loved me and did life with me for such a long time. It didn't matter. When you are doing what God put inside of you to do, you will have haters. You will have people who just don't understand, and how could they? God didn't tell them what He told you. Don't be driven by what others think. It's yours, and He gave you everything you need to make it through even the hurts and gashes from the people you love. This was a battle, and even one that I continue to this day even after so much goodness and abundance has flowed into my life.

Become available for God to move. Rest in the stillness and absorb the clarity that is already within you. Underneath the stuff stacked inside, beyond the fog you have created and within the feelings, desires, and passions that you were created with. Take a look at your motives.

For me, I found myself in the situation I was in because of the inaccurate beliefs I held my entire life. I learned that when those beliefs are your focus, then that becomes your reward. If you are pursuing your endeavors solely for the sake of money, then that will be your reward, and your life will be devoid of joy, happiness, peace, and meaningful relationships along the journey. If you are doing it for the car then that will be your reward. If you are doing it just to make it by paycheck to paycheck or just to have enough for retirement, then that will be your reward. If you are doing it out of real servanthood and desire to truly help people and change this world then that will be your reward. If you are doing it for God's glory then *that* will be your reward (and let me tell you, this is where "more than you could ever think or imagine" has the space to work and becomes evident in your life.)

What you focus on comes to you.

As I found myself in a place of financial distress, I began applying to various positions, awaiting the open door that I believed God intended for me. Soon, things began to shift. I received a call from the CEO of a company in my area, expressing interest in me as a potential new leader within their organization. With only one spot available, I felt a strong sense of drive towards this opportunity. I was convinced that this was where I belonged.

The process for securing this position was scattered and unorganized, spanning several weeks filled with meetings, walkthroughs, and numerous conversations, all with no clear agenda. As this seemingly perfect opportunity dragged out, I unexpectedly received an interview for a position back in the state I grew up in. This new opportunity would require me to move away from my children and the toxic environment I had found myself in. To my surprise, not only was I offered the interview, but the job posting was updated to include relocation assistance, covering the expenses of my move across the country. It was an astonishing alignment of events.

With interview dates set for both opportunities, I found myself faced with two vastly different potential job prospects.

Right before the holidays, when my emotional and financial stress was at its peak, the CEO of the local company called me and offered me the job. He was thrilled to have me and spoke very highly of everything I had done and said up to that point. He told me that he knew I would be a great fit to bring the company to the financial goals they had. I was relieved and ecstatic! I was a perfect fit, and I knew it from the beginning. This was the exact environment where I could thrive, and I was confident I could easily double this company's revenue, morale, and overall state in just a year. I had the blueprint. I had the plan.

My start date? The same day as my interview with the other company.

"Wow, this is nuts," I thought to myself. "Why can't God just give me one and let me know exactly what to do?"

He didn't.

I started this new job and completed the interview for the other opportunity on my lunch break that very first day.

The money at this new job was good, but I knew I would have to make some serious changes to get out of the financial mess that I put myself in. Even as I began the job, the CEO was thrilled with what I was doing. He called me a "breath of fresh air." It felt great to be appreciated and I knew something was still happening.

Not even a week later, I heard back from the other opportunity and got offered that job as well.

I had some decisions to make.

I talked with my middle son, who was living with me, and we both agreed that the right thing to do was to take the higher-paying job, which would allow us to move away to build better and away from the chaotic situation that I had been living in for a few years since my divorce. My son also decided that he wanted to go with me. He had been in the same muck and wanted to build a better life alongside me. So, we accepted the job, and I was going to continue at the local one I started until I had a firm start date and all was in order. That was my plan anyway.

When I came back to the office after New Year's weekend, I was getting everyone set up and dialed in for the plan of the day and the various meetings we had coming up. A colleague came in and said our CEO was on the phone and wanted to chat with us in his office.

"Be right there," I said.

A few minutes later I sat down in the boss's office and the CEO began to speak. It took a minute for what he was saying to sink in... He was letting me go.

What?! It had only been nine working days! What in the world?!

This was the very same CEO who was thrilled with me just days before and had been complimenting my work. Not to mention, he had not been in the office for a single day of my 9-day tenure there. The "reasons" he gave for my abrupt termination were ridiculous and even broke our employee agreement, but to me, it was confirmation that I had made the right choice.

A few weeks later my son and I were on the road back to Washington to start over.

Lots happened after this big move and again I looked for the lesson. The gift. What I realized is I needed to be away. I needed to be in a place where it was just me and God so He could show me who and where I was supposed to be. I longed to be back in Texas where we just came from – I never envisioned myself leaving my home there. I desperately wanted to reconcile some relationships and more than ever I wanted *His* purpose for my life – but there.

Still, in my heart, I felt Washington needed to happen. It was the place I needed to be. A sheep like I have never been before.

Only reliant on the shepard to guide me. He came through like He always does.

In a very short time abundance began to flow into my life. Ideas, old and new began flooding my spirit. Now was the time for these to take shape and become reality.

In fact, you are holding one of those dreams right now in your hands.

My life has become even more than I ever imagined and touched more lives than I ever thought possible since I have learned how to let go. The desires and passions have begun to unfold in ways only He could provide.

God has given us everything we need to bring to this world what He created us to do. My intention is to bring what He gave *me* and to encourage and pull out of *you* what He gave *you*.

This world needs *you*. This world needs me. This world needs God.

My mantra that I created years ago is, 'I am what this world needs.' This is not self-serving like, "I am God," or anything like that. It is to help me believe and remember that God created me for a reason. I have an influence and a platform that He made for my life to be an example and to show His power to this world.

You are what this world needs. You are what *your* world needs. You get this one life. What are you doing with it that truly brings change and help to those around you?

Are you stuck within vicious cycles of your own and destructive thought patterns that are keeping you down, just like I was the majority of my life?

You can break free. God can and will deliver you and break the chains binding you to these weights. What is driving you? Truly, deep down inside.

Is it limiting beliefs and selfish thinking? Is it your own pride, ego, or even narcissism?

Our past experiences help us make choices and find our way through life's ups and downs. They are like guiding lights that show us the way. You shouldn't dwell on the past; instead, you should learn from it. Every event gives us a chance to grow and change.

During all of this, it's important not to wallow in sorrow or feel sorry for yourself. Instead, enter every situation with an open mind, knowing that both good and bad things happen to you on your journey, and each one brings a lesson. A gift.

When we go deep within ourselves, we find insights that help us make better decisions and to act in ways that matter; and because we have faith, we know that even when things are hard, there is a plan and a purpose set aside for us.

Learn from the mistakes I've made and use those lessons to get through your own life with courage and strength.

We are paving the way for a legacy to be created.

Chapter 11: Unraveling It All

Our world needs a change, and it starts with you.

What choice will you make to ignite that change?

I believe so much in the power of *the* choice. The most powerful one of all that cannot be changed day by day. It is the one that you stand on even when you don't feel it, even when it's inconvenient or others disagree. A daily choice.

This choice is the one you make to live by your authentic truth, every single day, and it is one you can practice intentionally and literally, starting with your relationships with people.

Romantically, this means choosing the other person daily. Even if upset or hurt. Even if you try to convince yourself that you no longer love them. You made the choice, and you make it daily.

Choose to fight. Choose to stand.

Choose to set aside your greed and selfish ambitions for love. Choose to stand with the people you love against those trying to break you down and apart. Choose to stand for your world - both literally and figuratively, that you love and take it back.

My life and journey to finding my purpose wasn't about me. It was about God. It was always about showing that His love, power, and miracles are still alive and active today.

My hope for you is that today marks the beginning of your own journey, full of realizations, inspiration, and new ideas. Be driven by purpose. Let go of how you thought your life would go and align your desires with the divine. Stop flailing your arms trying to stay afloat and make yourself wholly available to the only one who can make your life greater and in ways far beyond what you could ever hope or imagine.

Don't give up. Don't give in. No matter how many times you have gotten it "wrong." Take it from me, who has failed countless times.

He's not done with me.

He's not done with *you*.

In the Bible there are many instances where God shows us the change that He can do within us. One of these stories roots way back: the story of Jacob. This story is a beautiful representation of the point that I am making and one that ultimately God is making over your life. Jacob represents the parts of you that you don't want anyone to see. The shadow side. The bad.

You see, God changed Jacob's name when he brought him into his true purpose and on multiple occasions still said, "I am the God of Jacob." He is telling us that even through our mess ups, our mistakes, our letdowns, our struggles, He is still our God. He is with us through it all and not just in victory or success. He is with us through the darkness and defeats. He is full of Grace and He's the God of Jacob too.

He's the God of Brandon too.

He is the God of my shadow side. The side of me that I don't want anyone to see or even know about. The side of me that I'm ashamed and embarrassed of. He loves me; he chose me. His purpose is greater than anything I could even build or force on my own. To find it I had to receive clarity that He is my God too and let go and allow Him to do what only He can do. It required me to unclench my fists and surrender; let go of what I thought and expected and even believed God for; shed all of my old self and in an organic way, not peel away frantically in my own ways; allow the process to work, stay out of the way, no matter how long it took; fall completely apart to have God put me back together in ways only He can and in ways that shine the light for all to see his works.

This is transformation.

The process can be a dagger to the heart and especially a *big* blow to your ego. Trust it anyway. I still believe there is a plan for my life even after all of the mess ups I have made and the chaos I have caused. My life can still bring healing to this world and encouragement for all.

"OH, LET THE BULLETS FLY, OH, LET THEM RAIN MY LIFE, MY LOVE, MY DRIVE, IT CAME FROM... PAIN!"

BELIEVER: IMAGINE DRAGONS

My life up until recently, as you hopefully are seeing, was driven by me. My way. Driving toward what I believed to be my purpose. Knowing that there was more and going after anything and everything to grab hold of a purpose – any purpose. The clarity came when I realized I was doing it all on my own. I was praying, I was seeking God, but I wasn't in tune; I wasn't in alignment. I was flailing.

I was fighting.

Now I am here with life, with freedom, with love and with drive. All of this came out and was birthed from my pain, from the paths that I took, and the realization that it was all me.

Let go. Get out of your own way.

This world has fallen apart and needs heroes. It needs people who are all in for their God-given purpose to find it through His grace. The strength to change the world is within us, but the process is not what society is advertising. We need soldiers to stand, sit, and kneel as sheep. To seek after the true plan for our lives and the world-changing power that we hold within us. This is the only way. This is how we make the difference we all feel within our hearts to make. This is how we truly help others and build a legacy that will outlast us.

This is how we are driven by His purpose.

This book may come across as jumbled. That's ok. I wanted to portray my mind and the battle I have been fighting.

What I want you to know is that you are not alone. This world seeks meaning and purpose. I seek meaning and purpose. The difference is, we know where it is found – not in the noise, but in the stillness.

Seek after the stillness. Fight for the quiet. Be violent in protecting the space where God speaks. Become available and present in His presence. This is where direction lies. This is where we understand the battle plan for the day. Only then can we be prepared to head out and know our orders. Only then can we know what movements and routes to take, understand humility and gentleness, and be aware of how we can not leave those around us behind or run over them in the process. It is where our hearts are opened to life and to love. In this place, we become the least, the servant of all, and that is where our reward lies.

Recognize that you are not the only one looking for meaning and purpose in life. Every soul is created for a purpose, craving for fulfillment and a sense of belonging that goes beyond the ordinary activities of daily existence. However, in the middle of the world's confusion, it is far too simple to become lost in the chorus of voices competing for our attention; all of them seem to offer some sort of meaning and truth.

We are frequently thrown into this sea of competing beliefs, trying to find a firm foundation to anchor our souls to. But do not be surprised; among all of this chaos, a ray of hope shines brilliantly, pointing the way to the waters of spiritual enlightenment and inner calmness.

Welcome this calling with eager and open hearts. Shine brightly, removing the fear and doubt-causing curtain that can hide our real mission. By doing this, we create a lasting legacy that proves the transformational power of grace.

May our lives serve as a living example of the infinite love and compassion of God, as well as the human spirit's eternal capacity to overcome hardship and radiate unwavering brilliance. May our legacies encourage future generations to pursue peace, to stand up for silence, and to shine their lights in a world that desperately needs them.

This world needs people who are available to be driven by His purpose.

Will that be you?

Finding the right way to end this book was a challenge for me but God brought it clearly. A way to summarize the points that have been made in a very simple yet powerful story. This journey takes place in Mark Chapter 5.

22 Then one of the synagogue leaders, named Jairus, came, and when he saw Jesus, he fell at his feet. 23 He pleaded earnestly with him, "My little daughter is dying. Please come and put your hands on her so that she will be healed and live." 24 So Jesus went with him.

35 While Jesus was still speaking, some people came from the house of Jairus, the synagogue leader. "Your daughter is dead," they said. "Why bother the teacher anymore?"

36 Overhearing what they said, Jesus told him, "Don't be afraid; just believe."

37 He did not let anyone follow him except Peter, James and John the brother of James. 38 When they came to the home of the synagogue leader, Jesus saw a commotion, with people crying and wailing loudly. 39 He went in and said to them, "Why all this commotion and wailing? The child is not dead but asleep." 40 But they laughed at him.

After he put them all out, he took the child's father and mother and the disciples who were with him, and went in where the child was. 41 He took her by the hand and said to her, "Talitha koum!" (which means "Little girl, I say to you, get up!"). 42 Immediately the girl stood up and began to walk around (she was twelve years old). At this they were completely astonished.

Jairus was a leader in his community and he was faced with a situation that brought great passion and drive to get God to take action. Jairus believed that God was the only way and he sought after it. He removed all else and became available. Not only did he seek Jesus out and humble himself by pleading for Jesus to take action, but he had a vision in his head of exactly what this healing would look like. This leader believed in God and had limiting beliefs on how this healing could happen.

It did not go the way he envisioned. The journey to the daughter took longer and the daughter died. What I want to say here is – do not wait until rock bottom.

Your promises and purpose can be found without it. In the midst of this chaos; Jesus responds with, "just believe." The promises and the purpose of your life are taking longer than you thought they would or they are unfolding in ways you never imagined that they would.

Just believe.

Jesus then takes his inner circle to the girl and even removes the crowd. Your inner circle has power when united. Find those people and remove the noise. Remove the negativity and the naysayers. Take out the things or even people in your life that are not adding true value. Stop inviting answers from people who are not on the same level as you, or who don't believe in where you want to go. The answers are found in the room with Jesus, not in the crowd.

Get in the room with the person who can make the miracles happen; who can bring those promises and purpose to life. The daughter was healed. Jesus came through, just not in the way that was expected or even asked for. The promises will be fulfilled. The purpose will be brought to light and aligned in ways you never imagined. People will be changed for the good along the way. You may not always see it every day but your life is a living example and people see it.

What are they seeing?

This world does not need a new definition of religion, the gospel, the good news or whatever else you want to refer to it as. We need a new *demonstration* of it. We need leaders to pray and walk in and be available for God's power to move here and now.

"No man is greater than his prayer life. The pastor who is not praying is playing; the people who are not praying are straying. We have many organizers, but few agonizers; many players and payers, few pray-ers; many singers, few clingers; lots of pastors, few wrestlers; many fears, few tears; much fashion, little passion; many interferers, few intercessors; many writers, but few fighters. Failing here, we fail everywhere."

-Leonard Ravenhill

We need you.

Keep believing, keep praying and keep moving.

9 798227 145079